AN EYE ON DESIGN

Paul Reilly

AN EYE ON DESIGN

An Autobiography

MAX REINHARDT

LONDON

For my darling Annette who has shared so much of my life and without whom this book would not have happened.

British Library Cataloguing
in Publication Data
Reilly, Paul
An eye on design.
1. Reilly, Paul 2. Design, Industrial –
Great Britain – Biography
I. Title
745.2′092′4 TS140.R4/
ISBN 0-370-31067-5

Printed in Great Britain for
Max Reinhardt Ltd
32 Bedford Square, London WC1B 3EL
by Butler & Tanner Ltd, Frome and London
Photoset in Ehrhardt by
Rowland Phototypesetting Ltd
Bury St Edmunds, Suffolk

First published 1987

CONTENTS

The author and publishers
wish to make the following acknowledgements:

Extract from *Room 39 Naval Intelligence in Action 1939–45* by Donald McLachlan reproduced by kind permission of David Higham Associates Ltd.

Extract from *All Things Bright & Beautiful* by Fiona MacCarthy reproduced by kind permission of Allen & Unwin.

Extract from a letter from Sir Francis Meynell to Paul Reilly, reproduced by kind permission of Dame Alix Meynell.

Extract from a speech made by HRH The Duke of Edinburgh, reproduced with his own kind permission.

While every effort has been made to trace the owners of copyright of the photographs, this has not proved possible in all cases.

ILLUSTRATIONS

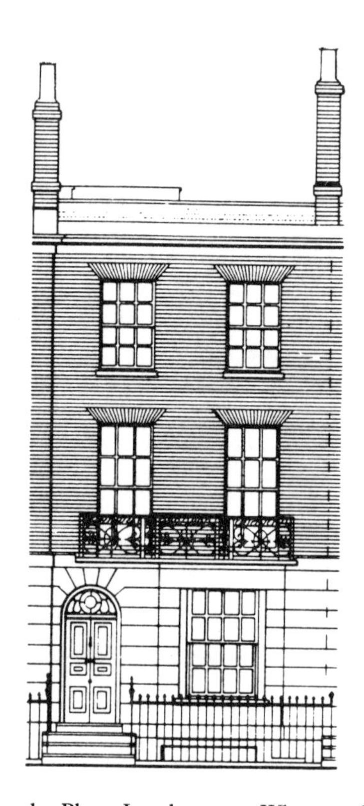

1. 3, Alexander Place, London SW7. Where we live now

1

Early Years

I was born in 1912 in Liverpool in a house called Dingle Bank. On three occasions since then I have had cause to recall the Dingle. The first was in 1938 when Gerald Barry, the editor of the *News Chronicle*, sent all his journalists back to their home towns to see what had happened to their birth places. Mine I discovered had been obliterated to make room for a vast oil storage park; I reckoned that Dingle Bank had stood about three tanks along in the third row up from the river.

The next occasion was at the Victoria and Albert Museum in 1975 when Roy Strong was staging his heartrending exhibition about the destruction of English country houses. As my wife and I reached the room in which a sepulchral voice was listing the losses county by county we suddenly heard Dingle Bank read out. From the catalogue it appeared that the house had been pulled down in 1919.

The last occasion was in 1983 when as a member of British Rail's Environment Panel I went back to Liverpool to see the site of the great Garden Festival planned to take place all over the oil storage park, which had been moved across the river. This time I reckoned Dingle Bank must have stood on the rising ground to be occupied by the international gardens, but memory is a poor guide, for I was only two when we left Dingle Bank. I do, though, recall the banana boats, those great white steamers tied up in mid-Mersey, waiting no doubt for their turn to dock; and I remember my father's first car, a small GWK (fifty miles per hour and fifty miles per gallon), though it may be his telling me of the car's prowess that I remember. But I do clearly recall my mother's farewell to my sister and me. We were both on our pots in the nursery, back to the fire, she on the right, me on the left, when my mother swept in hatted and coated and kissed us both and was gone. That was the last we saw of her for several years as she had contracted consumption and was an invalid on and off for the rest of her life. Her place was taken, so to speak, by a governess, a Miss Laker, who took my sister and me to stay in a boarding house in Hoylake near the golf course where we spent the rest of the war except for visits to my grandparents in Highgate and Upminster.

The Highgate house was a large mid-Victorian Italianate villa called The Eagles, after two cement birds on top of the gate piers. It had a fine garden in which its later owners, the Russian trade delegation, commissioned Eric Lyons to build a tower block to house their staff. I once took my daughter to Highgate to show her where her great-grandmother's family had lived, but we only got ten yards up the drive before a large black Zim limousine filled with large square Russians made us turn tail. But the sounds of the balalaika music had proved my point about the occupants.

The Upminster house was much older, a typical Essex village house with a Georgian façade stuck onto seventeenth-century hindquarters. It too had a splendid garden with a great Cedar of Lebanon dominating the gravel broad walk from my grandfather's study. It was a garden full of incident, with a nut walk, a serpentine red brick wall for peaches, a large shaggy mulberry tree that bore great bleeding fruit and a copse into which one Sunday afternoon a little aeroplane crash landed and the pilot, in smart Royal Flying Corps uniform, came to tea. He told us that a few days before he had taken part in the destruction of the first Zeppelin to be shot down. This meant a lot to me, for my sister and I had seen the great airship caught in the searchlights and then suddenly burst into flames; I was still drawing flaming Zeppelins with burning men jumping out. High House, as my grandfather's house was called, was the second largest in the village, the largest being Hoppy Hall where the Wedgwood Benns lived, but both are gone now. My father sold High House a year or two after my grandfather's death, the proceeds helping my unmarried aunt and uncle to survive.

But these three houses—Dingle Bank, The Eagles and High House—were all architecturally interesting and must all have influenced me. Dingle Bank was really the prettiest—a sort of Jane Austen house with a verandah and a marvellous view down its own grass to the river. I believe my architect father (who never earned more than £900 p.a.) did wonders with brown paper on his walls, black paint, and red cushions to sit on instead of chairs round a dining room table. The other rooms were more conventionally furnished, with excellent eighteenth-century pieces all of which were burnt in a Liverpool warehouse fire. I still possess one of my mother's paintings of herself and some children, including my elder sister Joanna who died from meningitis shortly afterwards, which gives a good impression of an Edwardian living room. My mother was a pupil of Professor Tonks at the Slade, a good pupil it would seem, because a knowledgeable friend of mine once saw the picture and congratulated me on owning a Tonks. It was a great pity that her illness was soon to put an end to her painting, though not to her drawing. She would spend hours in bed drawing, one of her favourite subjects being her left hand. She used to tell me that a human hand contained as much to draw as a whole body.

Our wartime spell at Hoylake was memorable for Miss Laker's beautifully polished brown shoes; for flying visits from my father who, having been a considerable sprinter at Cambridge, would take his son's hand and run with him incredibly fast; for batches of German prisoners of war, wearing not helmets but soft round caps; and, on Armistice Day, for a biplane which, having dropped its leaflets announcing peace, came down nose first on the golf course—it did not catch fire, but gave off a strong smell of aeroplane fuel, which became for me a firmly imprinted childhood memory. But my strongest memory of Hoylake, or perhaps it was of West Kirby, is my first experience of fear or fright. My father's youngest brother, my Uncle Arthur, who had been severely handicapped by meningitis as a boy and could not walk properly, came to see us. My father took us to a stretch of water enclosed by a low sea wall. Although the tide was coming in he thought we would have time to get round before the sea came over, but we had not calculated that Uncle Arthur would fall down every few paces. Half-way round my father realised we were in trouble for the sea water was already lapping over the wall. He ordered my sister and me to go on ahead; he would wait with Uncle Arthur. I was scared for my sister and myself as there was a lot of slimy green stuff under foot but we got round and then had a dreadful time watching Uncle Arthur and my father struggling to complete the course. They made it eventually with Uncle Arthur soaked to the skin and my father nearly as wet, but what had really frightened me was the thought that my father would drown trying to save his brother. This would have been a disaster, for I really owe what success I have had to my father.

The next three years were among the most formative of my early life. I was sent with my sister to a dame school in Uley, Gloucestershire. It seemed that every Reilly was at one time or another an inhabitant of that school, for I recall a great number of cousins being there. I think that we all followed in the footsteps of Patrick, the cleverest member of the family, who eventually became our Ambassador in Paris, after getting two firsts at Oxford and a fellowship at All Souls. The school was run by a Mrs Philips in an ancient gabled Cotswold house with plenty of garden and two yew trees which made good climbing. The day we arrived I met my first Americans, two brothers, who introduced me to the French Revolution by having arranged in our playroom a sort of guillotine, the blade being the lid of a box of toys. The Americans did not stay long, but in due course I became a keen student of the Revolution. The staff of the school included Mrs Philips' daughter, Olivia, Lance her shell-shocked son and an extraordinarily patient nanny-type called Anna Maria Louisa Higham. It was she who looked after the new arrivals. She slept just the other side of a wooden partition which did not reach the ceiling. I remember trying to pull myself up in order to squint at her from above, but I never caught her naked. There was, though, a teenager whose name I have properly forgotten, who very kindly let me into her bed, but in spite of a talk I had had with my father about the facts of life (he had felt it necessary to give me this since he was about to cross the Atlantic with my mother and thought that if their ship were to hit a mine he would at least have left me properly clued up) nothing happened for I was only six years old. And in any case I couldn't really believe him in view of the then mini-dimensions of my own parts. Another transatlantic passenger from Uley was a great friend of mine, a young gorilla called John Daniel, who used to play with us when his owner brought him to tea. We were all very sad when he left and even sadder when we learned his fate. He had died of sea-sickness before reaching New York. I used to have a small scar on my left wrist where he had playfully nipped me.

It must have been six years later, when I was twelve, that my father first inspired me to look at buildings. He took my sister and me to look at the chateaux of the Loire starting with the modest ones like Villandry with its splendid gardens and Cherverney, but ending with the great eye openers like Chenonceaux and Chambord. We stayed, I recall, in a small hotel in Tours and in a similar one at Blois, where I had a preview in the chateau courtyard of the staircase of my future Oxford college. It was about this time that my father extended my architectural education a bit further by taking us to Ghent, Bruges, Antwerp and Brussels, where I spent hours looking at the glories of the Grande Place and nearly as long no doubt marvelling at the impudence of the *mannequin pis*; and to Ostend, where I watched Pavlova dance.

I suppose that my years at Uley taught me what little I know about the countryside for we were taken on long walks up onto the Bury, the great flat-topped hill that shut out the view of the Severn valley, or round to Owlpen to see the haunted manor house surrounded by its yew trees carved into spectacular shapes. On fine days we would go on paper chases, the trail being laid by two of the older boys. On Sundays of course we went to church where I first heard those hymns—I could never sing them—which must recall childhood to the great majority of the English of my generation. My cousin Michael Reilly, who became a distinguished surgeon, and I tried to escape from Uley. We both had Meccano sets and thought that by uniting them we might even build ourselves an aeroplane and fly away over Bury Hill. We easily assembled a floor large enough for two small boys to stand on and then raised a vertical post with a hand operated propeller at the top. 'Supposing it works,' we said to each other, 'supposing it works.' Of course it didn't, but it gave us great pleasure to think of getting away from the Gables or perhaps from the food which was awful, particularly the dreadful date pudding.

My next school was a more serious affair, a proper preparatory school at Farnborough, Hampshire, run by two headmasters, Mr North, a large man with aquiline nose and black moustache, and Mr Ingram, a kindly, curly-haired man with a gentle voice which made our evening prayers quite pleasurable. I went to Farnborough, and to Winchester afterwards, because my cousin Patrick was already there. The school was well equipped with an indoor swimming bath, a chapel, four Eton fives courts, a fine flat playing field with a two-storeyed cricket pavilion and, all round the edge of the field, trees and bushes in which we used to build nests and hideaways and in which one of the older boys showed me his maturity by masturbating. It was a great cricketing school, our heroes belonging to the Crawley family—L.G., Cosmo, Aidan and Kenneth—but it was also quite distinguished academically with several scholarships or exhibitions every year to places like Eton, Harrow or Winchester. These successes were largely due to a former headmaster, a Mr Cumberbatch, who stayed on as the teacher of the top form; he retired, alas, before I got there, but I vividly remember his Christmas term ghost stories.

2. Dingle Bank, Liverpool. My birth place

3. High House, Upminster, Essex. My grandfather's house

4. Fancy dress No. 1 – as a student in Germany

5. Fancy dress No. 2 – as a trooper in the Royal Armoured Corps

6. Fancy dress No. 3 – as an RNVR officer in Holland

He would gather the whole school—all fifty-eight of us—together in the library, turn out the lights and, speaking without notes or hesitation, tell the most hair-curling stories. The master to whom I owed most was Mr Clewes who, besides supervising our cricket, taught us history and made the lessons infinitely interesting by illustrating through his magic lantern the clothes, furniture and architecture of each period. His lessons were my first introduction to what was to become my life's work, for they demonstrated that one can learn about design without doing, without practising a craft; the eyes are as important as the hands. His geography lessons were illustrated in the same way, clothing and buildings being revealed as we circled the globe.

By contrast with my next school, I was rather bright at Farnborough. I think I ended up head of the school, wearing three caps for cricket, soccer and rugby football, and I won two pewter mugs for fives, nasty curvaceous little things typical of many English trophies. I certainly enjoyed my five years there and learned a lot, to judge from the notebooks which I still have in which I had to draw as well as write. I discovered later on that many of the drawings were taken from *The Story of Mankind* by Hendrik van Loon, a book given to me by my mother. The main advantage of going to a school like Farnborough, particularly for a boy with few contacts, was the opportunity to meet some of the sons of the famous, most of whom seemed destined for Eton or Harrow, or else to get to know boys who were going to be famous like Kenneth Younger or Aidan Crawley. I remember the first words that Aidan Crawley addressed to me in the swimming pool where we all swam naked. He was standing next to me and looking at my stomach said, 'Where did you get that pot belly from?'—the first time I became aware of my unfortunate shape which I have been trying to cope with ever since that fearfully hot summer of 1921, when the cricket pitches dried up and cracks appeared in the playing field. The school, which was a large mid-nineteenth-century stuccoed building, from the top floor of which we practised fire drill by going head-first down a chute, now no longer exists. I did drive in once to find it razed to the ground, chapel and swimming pool and all, with only the crumbling fives courts still standing, but the playing field was still there, though now surely built over. The school stood just across the road from the Royal Aeronautical Establishment from which came at frequent intervals the roar of aeroplane engines being tried out.

My father was always convinced that I got into Winchester thanks to the happy accident of my opening a door to let my sister through instead of rushing on ahead of her. We were staying at the Bourne Hall Hotel in Bournemouth where we were visited by Mr H. A. Jackson (the Jacker), the house master of 'B' house, who had come to inspect me and possibly my father too. Apparently, when the interview was over and my sister and I were on the way out, the Jacker swivelled round in his chair to watch us leave, to judge, as my father said afterwards, whether manners would make this man. Fortunately they did and I was accepted, though I'm sure the real reason was that Patrick was already in the Jacker's house and doing very well, so perhaps he thought another Reilly would add some more lustre. Alas he did not for, except for winning the Holgate Divinity Prize and the Silver Kirby Foils, I had a very dim career at Winchester. Patrick on the other hand became head of the school, Senior Commoner Prefect and won a scholarship to New College, Oxford. But as the years have gone by, I have become fonder in retrospect of Winchester, whether because of the cathedral, where the school had infrequent services, or of the deanery and close, or of our own chapel or of chantry and its mediaeval cloisters; even now I like Sir Herbert Baker's War Memorial Cloisters. Yet I was obviously pretty unhappy there to start with for I wrote every day of my first year to my mother and she kept the letters which I have gladly destroyed.

We had a sensible custom at the school whereby a boy in his second year was appointed to look after a new boy and steer him through his 'notions', those strange words which had survived from earlier generations, some of them being Chaucerian. In my day there was a book of notions, published in hardback, which one was supposed to know by heart. I had taken mine on my first journey abroad to Paramé, near St Malo, where my mother and I walked up and down the beach struggling to master the strange vocabulary. My TJ (short I believe for protégé) was a kind and helpful chap called Markham, who eventually went into the Church and became a canon, if not something more, so I passed all right, but then had to face being 'beaten out of sweating', a painful ordeal now abolished. It involved running naked six times round the largest dormitory and being beaten or flicked with wet towels by the six prefects.

My great handicap at Winchester was my size. I was about the smallest boy who had ever gone there, so small that I was still wearing an Eton collar on Sundays in my third year when most boys had got rid of theirs after their first one, so small that I was once locked in a chest of drawers and beaten for missing chapel and so small that my father had to promise me a pill that was advertised to add at least six inches to a person's height. Perhaps that did the trick, for I eventually began to grow without the pill, but they were anxious days. I think perhaps it was my fencing that started my growth. It certainly took the Jacker's attention away from my abysmal performance on the cricket and football fields, though I was a keen spectator of Winchester football from my first term when I watched R. H. S. Crossman in the college team; he seemed bigger than life with enormous thighs; he was also Prefect of Hall and read the lessons in chapel—a man for whom my admiration started early.

My father was very ambivalent about Winchester. He swore that he would de-Wykehamise me in the holidays and poked constant fun at any indication that what he was paying for was having any effect, so much so that I was always very nervous when he put in an appearance. I remember one occasion when my house was drilling for the Officers' Training Corps I suddenly saw him approaching us accompanied by the Jacker. When he was well within earshot I heard him say loudly to the Jacker, 'Why is Paul in the back row?' I got out of the OTC as soon as possible thereafter and joined the Scouts, but not until I had failed Cert. A, a feat which won me a telegram of congratulations from my father.

I was also very nervous when my father came to lecture to the whole school in the famous Wren building, for I think he was as nervous as I was, but it all passed off without embarrassment. Many years later I too suffered a similar anxiety when I had to lecture in the post-war assembly hall designed by my father's old pupil, Sir Peter Shepheard. At this time we were again living in Liverpool at No 71 Bedford Street—a long journey from Winchester, but one which the two Liverpudlians at the school, Nicholas Monsarrat, the son of a Liverpool dentist, and I managed very well since there was a train which went direct to Birkenhead from where we crossed the river by ferry. We first made this journey together from the sanatorium where a few boys had been kept behind with measles or something, and where I fell in love for the first time with a splendid red-haired Irish nurse who taught me how to kiss.

The headmaster at this time was a wonderful long-legged priest called the Reverend A. T. P. Williams who could be seen most afternoons striding off with his stick and his crumpled felt hat across Meads and on towards St Catherine's Hill—that hill which in my day was smooth of flank and crowned of summit, but which later became covered with thorn bushes and almost bald on top. One day to my astonishment he asked me to go with him, a walk I shall always remember, for he encouraged me to join the school archaeological society and to have a shot at an Oxford scholarship; and those two pieces of advice came together and ended by my winning an exhibition to Hertford College, Oxford, since one of my history questions was to trace the growth of the English country house—the very subject on which two weeks before I had addressed the archaeological society. And then, having won my exhibition, I was told by the headmaster to stop ordinary work and instead to read the *Manchester Guardian* every morning and discuss what I had read with Professor R. M. Y. Gleadowe every afternoon, a duty which I at least greatly enjoyed for he was the art master, whose little empire was the room above chantry whither the very few boys who wanted to draw would repair. Gleadowe eventually became the Slade Professor at Oxford and the craftsman of the Stalingrad Sword. He was, though, too good a draughtsman to be a good teacher, or so it seemed to me, for he would set us the most impossible tasks like drawing a bird's eye view of the college from the chapel roof, a thing he could do with his eyes shut. So when I went on to Oxford, an even richer field for a good draughtsman, I threw in the sponge and gave up trying to draw and thus did not succeed my father and grandfather but left it to my sister to become the architect. Oxford, however, had plenty to offer in other fields.

My first visit to Oxford was to Trinity College which with its Wren chapel and Georgian buildings seemed to me to be perfection, as it still does. I was hoping to get a scholarship there, but failed; instead I was invited to Hertford College and for an interview from which it was quite clear to me that my answer on the English house had appealed to someone. I did, though, go through the most awful trauma at the interview for I was asked what books I had read recently. I said *The Case of Sergeant Gricka* and almost immediately realised that it was my father who had read it not I—too late, they began to question me on it and I had to own up.

During my first evening at Oxford there was a knock on my door and a man with a strong Liverpool accent introduced himself as Leslie Brewer and sat down until about three a.m. He was a great talker and I learned almost all I needed to know about Hertford College from that first conversation. It was also, for an Old Wykehamist, quite a good introduction to life at Oxford. The principal of the college, the historian Crutwell, also tried to arrange a special introduction for me. He asked me early in my first term to Sunday lunch, there to meet the two most eccentric figures in the college, wearing the strangest clothing and talking their heads off, whereas I was in my tweeds and quite tongue-tied. When I later asked Crutwell about the lunch party he said he had had a letter from my housemaster warning that Reilly's problem would not be wine or women if you see what I mean, so Crutwell thought he would try me out. How little the Jacker knew of me.

My three years at Oxford were among the happiest that I have spent. The days were filled with friends of both sexes, some of them beautiful like Sheila Grant-Duff, Iona Craig or Diana Hubback, some of them interesting like Michael Foot or Tony Greenwood, but all of them riveting. Sheila and Diana were particular friends of Adam von Trott zu Soltz, the very clever, handsome German undergraduate who, to the surprise of all who knew him at Oxford, joined the Nazis, but eventually took part in the von Stauffenberg plot to kill Hitler and was executed most foully by being hanged from a meat hook. In spite of a difficult beginning, I made the Oxford Union Society, rather than my college, the centre of my life, either because of the weekly debates or the honey buns for tea. My father had always been exceedingly ambitious for me where the Union was concerned. He made me promise to speak there; indeed he said he would only make up my exhibition if I did speak. One term went by—no speech; a second term—no speech, but a severe talking to in the vacation; half way through the third term a telegram: 'I meant what I said about the Union.' I knew then that unless I did speak that would be my last term, so I sought out Geoffrey Wilson the president and told him my problem. 'Excellent', he said, 'I will call you next week. It will be a good subject for you.' The debate was to be on town planning. I spent hours putting my speech together and, heart in mouth, went along to the debate. Imagine my horror to hear my name called out immediately after the paper speeches when the house was still full and my further horror to be interrupted after a couple of sentences. I gave way, found something to say in reply and then dried up. I could not even read what I had written, so sat down. To my astonishment the two university magazines reported quite favourably on me, one of them even suggesting that I was future presidential material, but I knew better. The episode gave me such a horror of speaking in public that it was some twenty years before I did it again. But I had spoken in the Union and my father kept his word. I was not cut off. My father's ambition for his son never left him. On my twenty-first birthday I got a telegram from him. It read, 'Congratulations. Four years more.' I could not think what he meant, until it dawned on me that William Pitt was Prime Minister at twenty-five. My father, though a successful architect and a great professor of architecture, was always a politician manqué. He was quite fearless on his feet. He was also a Fabian and co-sponsor with Ramsay MacDonald and Sir Oswald Mosley of the socialist 1917 Club. He thus managed to persuade all manner of public speakers to visit Liverpool and his school of architecture, among them being the father of my best friend at Oxford with whom I eventually shared digs. This was Arthur Greenwood who told his son Tony to seek me out.

Tony Greenwood was at Balliol and exactly my contemporary. I learned a lot from him. We joined the Labour Club together and danced with Barbara Betts, later Barbara Castle. He became President of the Union. We were both reading Modern Greats. I did a little better than he did, ending up with a second, at which my father could not bring himself to speak to me for about three weeks. He had got a first at Cambridge and Patrick Reilly had already got his two firsts at Oxford, for which my father, being better known in England than his brother in India, got the congratulations. Tony was a virgin at Oxford and so was I; we were dead keen to change this state of affairs and this gave us plenty of scope for comparing notes. I kept in touch with Tony over the years and was glad to find him in the House of Lords when my turn came. He had had a distinguished career in the Commons becoming Minister of Housing in Harold Wilson's government; this office once brought him to the Design Centre to open one of our exhibitions. I became godfather to his daughter Susannah, but had earlier introduced him to his striking blond wife. I took him as a young man to stay the weekend at Tufton Manor near Whitchurch which was inhabited by four couples, all of them concerned with the arts and design—Ashley and Margaret Havinden (he a leading graphic artist, she a director of Crawfords advertising agency); Wells Coates and his current girl friend (he the best known modern architect); Johnny Duncan Millar and wife (he a successful interior designer, who eventually became *The Times* correspondent in Washington); Walter and Jill Goetz (he the draughtsman of 'Colonel Up and Mr Down', a strip cartoon that ran for years in the *Daily Express*, she the excellent window dresser for Jaegers). It was Jill whom Tony eventually married. She became in later life an extremely good water colourist. We are proud to possess one.

My other good friend at Oxford was Michael Foot, a year younger than me and not yet a socialist, but already a formidable debater. He too, of course, became President of the Union. He was also President of the Lotus Club of which I was secretary. The Lotus Club was an Anglo-Indian Club numbering about fifty, twenty-five Indians and twenty-five Englishmen. We dined once or twice a term in an hotel in Cornmarket. In 1931 Gandhi came to London for the Round Table Conference so I invited him to dine with us. He accepted and brought his son who was formally dressed while he wore his dhoti. After dinner we went to Humayun Mirza's rooms in Queens. He was the son of the Diwan of Mysore and a very generous host who would press me time and again to visit him in India. I never did, but would instead steer all my Indian friends to call upon my uncle, Sir Darcy Reilly, the Chief Justice of Madras, who in turn would complain to his elder brother, my father, asking whether he could persuade his son to desist. I did not realise the embarrassment that my introductions would cause to someone so senior in our Indian Civil Service.

When I got to Oxford I found my way to the fencing club where 'Sammy' Cromarty-Dickson presided. He was an admirable instructor, with a keen sense of duty. His great ambition was always to win the university match and he would urge his team either to sleep with a girl the night before or take a double sherry immediately before. I went in for the university championship in my first year and came out on top in foils and so had to have a place in the Oxford side, thus finding myself fighting Neil Abercrombie, the son of Professor Patrick Abercrombie, my father's friend and colleague; 'A Reilly Foils an Abercrombie' was the *Liverpool Post*'s headline after the match. I held the half blue for all my time there. At one point I was appointed by my friend Tangye Lean, then editor of *Isis*, as the magazine's fencing correspondent and, as he was also a keen fencer, I had to challenge him to a duel. He had printed my only self-congratulatory report of a match against Bertrands, in which I had done rather well, under my own signature. We stripped to the waist and used *épées* and I drew the first blood, but much less than I was to see in Germany, whither Tony Greenwood and I went in the summer of 1932. We went to Marburg-an-der-Lahn to learn the little German required for our degree and stayed with a Frau von Pritzelwitz while we enrolled at the university.

Also staying with Frau von Pritzelwitz was Mr Wedgwood Benn, later Lord Stansgate, who had very recently been Secretary of State for India. He was learning German very fast and encouraged Tony and me to do the same but we had other distractions—for instance Frau von Pritzelwitz's daughter; the rising tide of Nazism; the Socialist Party's opposition called the Iron Front; and the outlawed Scharfe Mensur. Frau von Pritzelwitz's daughter rightly decided that the three young Englishmen—there was a third, the son of the Bishop of Dover—were not serious propositions, but we were taking the political problems with all seriousness. We joined the Iron Front and sported the Front's badge—three silver arrows—in our lapels and we went out at night with white chalk and crossed out every swastika we could see with three arrows. But the Nazis had more chalk and more men, well attended as were the Iron Front meetings. There seemed to be little opposition to our membership of the Iron Front, either in the von Pritzelwitz household or in the Marburg University classroom where we struggled with economics lectures in German. But before that summer's election the German public had not really made up its mind. It was still safe not to be a Nazi.

In July 1932 Tony and I went to Cassel together with a young German called Schumann. In the train Tony began whistling the 'Internationale', when four brown shirts got into our carriage. We understood enough German to know that there would be some trouble at the next station, Cassel, so we were ready to be thrown out with our bags at our destination. Cassel was a strange town in those days—half the houses seemed to be flying Nazi flags and half red ones. We went with Schumann to his polling booth and he held up his card to show us that he had voted Socialist, though we had hardly returned to Oxford when we got a pathetic letter from him praising Hitler and berating all contributors to the Iron Front. We decided not to reply.

On the morning after the election we went into Cassel and particularly into those areas where the communist and Iron Front flags had been flying. They had all been replaced by swastikas. Nonetheless I can say in all honesty that the first anti-Nazis I met were Germans, just as I can say that the first blood that I saw let was German. I had joined a student corporation which entitled me to a *mutze* or student cap and also gave Tony and me access to a bout of duelling which was still a forbidden pursuit. We therefore had to get up very early and walk about five miles out of Marburg to an inn, the large upper room of which had been cleared of furniture and its floor sprinkled thickly with sawdust. Downstairs medical students in white coats were arranging their equipment behind a large window through which those not fighting could judge the behaviour of those undergoing facial surgery, for the whole purpose seemed to be to prove one's courage; and of course to leave with a well-placed gash across a cheek and for preference across a lip too. To ensure the scars lasted a lifetime, the medical staff dabbed salt into the wounds before stitching them up. It got very hot upstairs for the room was overcrowded, and very smelly as the blood flowed and congealed in the sawdust, and after a while I began to feel faint and made for the door. As I stumbled out I tripped over a prostrate body and looking down found Tony had already fainted. Not a good score for the English, but it provided me with my first article for a newspaper since my father sent my letter describing the affair to the editor of the *Manchester Guardian* who, on my return, invited me to turn it into a piece for publication.

Fencing, of a very different sort, provided me with the opportunity to get to know Sir Oswald Mosley, at that time not a fascist but the leader of the New Party. He organised a team to tour the public schools and asked me to join it. On the train journeys we talked mainly about politics. He seemed particularly interested to know what my generation thought of him. He was a good fencer, but a bad loser. I was to see him under very different circumstances in a few years' time.

On my return to England I was astonished to find liberal journalists like A. J. Cummings and Vernon Bartlett writing that Hitler was a good influence for peace in Europe, for Tony and I had got exactly the opposite impression, not only from talking with German students, but from watching the brown shirts marching, an impression that was reinforced a few years later when as a journalist myself I attended the Parteitag at Nuremberg and saw the massive parade with Hitler taking the salute.

For my first two years at Oxford, Hertford College was unable to offer tutorials in Politics or Economics, so those reading PPE had to go outside. I was fortunate enough to be sent to G. D. H. Cole for Politics and to John Maud for Economics, both of them dons at University College. I was to come across John Maud at various stages of his very distinguished career, the last occasion being on my first day in the House of Lords. Room had been made for me on the front cross bench next to Lord Redcliffe Maud, as he had then become. Suddenly a division took place and I, not knowing what to do, turned to him. 'Follow me—as usual,' he said, so I found myself voting against the Government and was upbraided for doing so on my first day by a junior minister who asked me how I dared. At Oxford John was full of fun; he told me half seriously that, since economics was not his subject, he had to mug to keep one lesson ahead of me—a very different state of affairs from my next tutor, for Hertford managed to attract J. E. Meade, the future Nobel Prize winner and Professor of Economics at Cambridge, but he arrived a little too late for me to benefit, even though I had learned J. M. Keynes's *Money Credit and Commerce* almost by heart.

2

Changing Jobs

Coming down from a university in 1933 was much like coming down in 1983. Jobs were very scarce. I began to be sorry not to have worked harder nor to have read something that would keep the wolf from the door. A second in PPE was not likely to be very appealing to an employer, as I was soon to discover. I had interview after interview to no avail. I was failed by ICI, Unilever, Pilkingtons and Tootall Broadhurst Lee—the last two providing passages of some interest. At Pilkingtons I was put through my first intelligence test, one feature of which involved adding up a long column of figures against a stop watch held just behind my head. The watch had a very loud tick which was all I could count in the time allowed, so I failed. Kenyon Jones, the Welsh rugby player, was, I recall, taken on, though he did not stay in glass. I came across him later as Chairman of Ronson. I was in later life to have many meetings with the Pilkingtons, Harry, Alistair and Antony, the last one with Harry, then Lord Pilkington, when as Chancellor of Loughborough University he presented me with an Honorary Doctorate of Science; as he did so he leaned forward and whispered, 'Had you joined us, you would never have got this.'

I had real hopes of my interview with Sir Kenneth Lee, for he was a friend of my father. I remember dressing rather smartly in a new grey overcoat and walking along the corridor of the Manchester train in order to get out of a first-class carriage—a tip I had been given by someone as a sort of morale booster. So out I stepped straight into a small crowd of hand-clapping Mancunians. It was not until the journey back, after yet another failed interview, that I learned what had happened. The man opposite me in the dining car began laughing as he was reading his evening paper which he pushed across to me saying, 'that must have been funny.' I read a headline, 'Mr Randolph Churchill arrives—mistaken identity comedy at station.' It then described my getting out of a first-class carriage and my smart grey coat. I wished I had known that he was on the train for I had been in the Oxford Union for the King and Country debate and the following week for Randolph Churchill's rape of the minute book, both of which created quite a stir in the press. When, many years later, I did meet him at an exhibition in New York, he was too busy searching for a drink for me to remind him of the episode. Obviously I must have a face that is easily mistaken for others', for on a train to Liverpool many years later an Irish waitress seized my hand and kissed my ring saying, 'You are the archbishop, aren't you?' Many people at that time of my life told me that I was the double of Archbishop Ramsey; even my wife used to say so, until one day at a party at St Bartholomew's I saw him and went over and stood by him so that Annette could see the difference.

My next interview was arranged by my father with his old friend and co-director Mr John Spedan Lewis. He was sitting behind a desk which had a bust of Napoleon on it. He appeared to be a large man until he stood up. He asked me in what subject I had got my first—at that time the John Lewis Partnership would only engage men and women with first-class degrees. On my confessing to my second, he said, 'Were you first class at anything?' I said, 'Yes, I got a fencing half blue,' to which he said, 'Only half a blue?' The interview ended by my being offered the post of fencing instructor to the partnership, the first of the three partnership posts he was eventually to offer me, the others being editor of partnership journalism, following a letter I had written to *The Times*, and advisor to the partnership on plastics, following my time in the United States on Modern Plastics.

Having failed to get a job, I decided, with my father's encouragement, to become self-employed. I got hold of a reference book to the world's press and extracted a list of all journals published in the British Empire—something over three hundred. I then registered the name Pall Mall Agency and its address as being in Whitcomb Street. Actually the address was in the typewriting office of my second cousin, Mary Reilly, who was going to gain a little—or a lot—from my venture. The plan was that I should write and Mary Reilly should have typed and duplicated about three thousand words a week, but first I had to sell the project. I therefore wrote a dummy letter with a covering one claiming that my contributors would include various well-connected recent graduates like Tony Greenwood and Michael Foot and offering the three thousand words for some ludicrously low figure to each of the three hundred or so papers. The weekly letter would cover all topics from politics to the arts, much of it drawn from material that had already appeared in the English press, but always re-written, on the advice of William Mellor, the editor of the *Daily Herald*. I made a sliding scale of charges so that if a paper subscribed for, say, three years it would get the weekly London letter for only ten shillings a week. One paper in India, the *Jayaji Pratap*, did this and translated me into Urdu, but the others were more cautious. At the final count, far from reaching three figures as I had hoped, I had only thirty takers, but widely spread from the Antigua *Magnet* to a Bulawayo Sunday paper. At any rate it was good practice if rather wearing, particularly in the third year when there was only the one Indian paper still subscribing, but I regarded myself as contracted; the others had one by one dropped out mainly for political reasons. I suppose this little venture did me no harm. It was nice to be a journalist, even a self-employed one, and it did enlarge my acquaintanceship. For instance it brought me in touch with Stephen King Hall, who was also producing a weekly typescript news letter and offered me a partnership, which I foolishly turned down. It also enabled me to get, in return for a favourable review, an inscribed copy from H. G. Wells of his *Shape of Things to Come.* Its most useful lesson was, however, the importance of deadlines. In three years I never missed my weekly posting.

With the income from the Pall Mall Agency I took myself to the London School of Economics and joined the first year of their business administration course under the direction of an American called Jules Mencken, who reported to that remarkable man Professor Arnold Plant, whom I was to meet some thirty years later. He then greeted me (I was by that time white and bald) with, 'Hello Reilly—Business Administration 1935.' He was only one year out; it should have been 1934. There were about twenty of us on the course which was modelled on the Harvard Business Administration one in that the backbone of Jules Mencken's course was the case study method. I believe it was wound up after two or three years—a great pity, for Britain had to wait for a long time to have another business school. The members of that first year all got jobs through having studied the problems set by those firms supporting the course, as on Saturday mornings we turned ourselves into a sort of company board. Our chairman was a member of the company that had set the problem. Apart from the introductions which this course gave us to a great number of firms in Britain, it taught me the art of report writing, a skill which would stand me in good stead later on.

I got my first job partly through the London School of Economics and partly through the Pall Mall Agency. I decided to use one of my last sheets of Pall Mall Agency paper for a letter to Venesta Limited, claiming that I represented an advertising agency with first-class architectural contacts—there was at least nothing on the letter paper to suggest otherwise. It fell into the hands of Jack Pritchard, the advertising manager to whom the name Reilly was not unknown, and he replied to say that he would call round to the Whitcomb Street office for a talk. I never expected that. I thought I would

7. Prince Charles and his panel of judges for the first Tarian

8. Lord Snowdon with the first four editors of *Design* magazine: Alec Davis, Michael Farr, Corin Hughes Stanton, John Blake

9. Antony Armstrong Jones arriving at The Design Centre on 23 January, 1961

be summoned to Venesta at Vintry House. However I persuaded my cousin to stay out of sight and to allow me to use her front room.

When Jack Pritchard arrived he said at once, 'I see you're looking for a job, aren't you?' I agreed and then told him about the LSE to which he said that Venesta was a sponsoring company and had set a problem. He urged me to take it seriously, which I did, with the result that they offered me a job, or at least Jack did, and I found myself within weeks working for a very rare man, one of the tiny minority of Britons who was aware of what was happening in European architectural circles and was eager to see Britain catch up. But first I had to complete my time at the LSE which, as it involved our working with the National Institute for Industrial Psychology, meant being sent to factories to write reports on them. A factory which I had to go to in Tottenham was the vast furniture one of Harris Lebus; it quite understandably eventually went out of business, as all such should. But at that time it was not my job to comment on design, but rather on the working conditions, which seemed excellent. My report earned me an interview with Sir Herman Lebus, the first of many that I was to have with members of that family.

By a strange coincidence, Jack Pritchard was also to spend some time at Lebus after the war. When I joined him at Venesta, however, he had just commissioned Le Corbusier to design Venesta's stand at the Building Trades Exhibition at Olympia and was in the process of commissioning Wells Coates to design the next one, on which I was to spend a week as a salesman. Some forty years later I was to find myself a non-executive director of Building Trades Exhibitions Limited. My job at Venesta was, to start with, of the dreariest kind—that of an order clerk—though before entering head office I had to spend some time in the Silvertown factory making toothpaste tubes and veneering flush doors; but as future head office material I was allowed to eat in the managers' canteen. When Jack Pritchard decided to leave Venesta to start his own Isokon furniture business his job was divided into two—the advertising going to Fred Oppé, the sales to me. Fred and I had met under the strangest circumstances. On my first day at Vintry House I had slipped up to Piccadilly Circus for lunch. There was one table left with only one man sitting at it. I asked permission to share and we got talking. He told me that it was his first day in his office. I said, 'ditto.' He had come west for lunch. 'Ditto.' His firm sold plywood. 'Ditto.' It was called Venesta. 'Ditto.' He was working for Jack Pritchard. 'Ditto.' We have been good friends from that day. I became a sales manager through the intervention of the joint managing director who sent for me one day and told me that he was going to make me sales manager of the building uses department and to prove his point called me over to his corner window and pointing down to the street below said, 'Do you see that policeman down there?' 'Yes Sir.' 'Well you can make him sole agent for our doors and panelling if you think he would sell more of them—that is how free your hand will be.' He also gave me a small rise, so I left his room rather pleased with myself, but perhaps sorry to give up my first job of calling upon architects, an activity that had reached my father's ears through someone asking him whether I was all right; it seemed that some of his professional colleagues were worried that I had become an alcoholic or some kind of drop-out. My father did not tell me this until I was safely employed elsewhere, so I went on knocking on the doors of his friends or of my contemporaries, among whom were Christopher Nicolson and Hugh Casson, the first partnership on which I left my card. I suppose that Michael Rosenauer was my best customer since he was putting up a great many blocks of flats like Arlington House Piccadilly and Troy Court, Kensington, and I sold him hundreds of doors. I was, though, more interested in calling upon modern architects like Frederick Gibberd and Wells Coates, different as they were from each other and different as was their architecture. I called upon Gibberd when he was working on Pullman Court, Streatham, not to my mind a good piece of architecture, but a great consumer of flush doors; indeed successful as Freddie became, I never warmed to his architecture, other than to what he did at Harlow. Wells was then designing Lawn Road flats—his client being Jack Pritchard—a building made almost entirely of ferro-concrete and Venesta plywood. I was eventually to live in the Isokon block, where I came upon many people of interest. There was, for instance, W. J. Brown, MP, who said to me once that when Churchill went there would be Beaverbrook, but when he went there would only be me; there was Walter Gropius, into whose two-roomed flat my wife and I moved when he went to America; there was Leslie Howard, the actor with whom I discussed a series of wartime films built around the inhabitants of a block of flats; there was Egon Riss, the Austrian architect, who had the idea of flooding the Channel with petrol ready for firing; and there was Marcel Breuer, the German architect who designed the Isokon furniture for Jack Pritchard.

Before changing jobs I had the pleasure of selling some bird's-eye maple panelling to Constance Cummings and her playwright husband Ben Levy for their bathroom in the modern house in Old Church Street, Chelsea, which they had commissioned from Maxwell Fry and Gropius. I tried unsuccessfully to get some of our plywood into the neighbouring house by Serge Chermayeff and Eric Mendelsohn, two famous architects, both good friends of mine who ended up in America. It would have been very nice to have had Venesta plywood in the two most modern houses in London.

My new job involved my travelling all round the country calling upon timber merchants. I had decided to reorganise our system of discounts which needed quite a lot of selling. As my expense allowance was very modest I stayed at small commercial travellers' (I had joined the union) hotels and thus came across the age-old ritual of the single table with the oldest traveller at the top, and the writing room where we wrote up our reports. I am glad to have had that experience.

But my time at Venesta was drawing to a close. I had taken a girl-friend to the sea at Littlehampton and on the pier I had paid a bob to have my hand read. The woman told me that I was doing something in the City and the job did not suit me. I would receive an invitation to join a London newspaper. It would come soon and out of the blue. 'My advice would be to take it,' she said. And come it did, a few weeks later. Tangye Lean rang me from the *News Chronicle* to say that there was a very small job going—assistant to the leader page editor—and would I like to be considered. Remembering Littlehampton, I said yes and in due course had my interview with Gerald Barry, the editor, who on my assuring him that I was curious, that I was consumed with curiosity, that is, appointed me. It was a very poorly paid job. I dropped three pounds a week to leave Venesta, but I entered a much more interesting world. Indeed I was plunged right in, for on my first day there was half a leader page to be filled by the ornithological correspondent, who failed to turn up, so I had to get the cuttings and write the piece on the migration of birds. That was my first introduction to the cuttings library, an invaluable institution upon which we all relied. A little later on I wrote an article on short wave diathermy, having been treated for a boil by my doctor, and received an enormous post bag, most of the letters being addressed to Doctor Reilly.

The assistant to the leader page editor was well placed to learn a lot about the newspaper for he had to run between the editorial floor and the case room, taking copy up and bringing proofs down, sometimes cutting to length on the stone and always telegraphing the layout and content of the page to Manchester, where the paper was also printed. When I joined, Tangye Lean was the leader page editor, reporting to Ralph McCarthy, the features editor, a very busy man who had a habit of touring his offices every day, asking the same questions, 'Are you happy?' and 'Any ideas?' I think he was rather impressed by having two Oxford graduates reporting to him for Tangye, at least, was an arrogant, awkward customer, who delighted in aggravating McCarthy, much to my advantage, for McCarthy was a real professional newspaperman who was glad to share his experience with an amateur. I thus not only learned a great deal, but was also given bits to write on other pages. The *News Chronicle* was generous to its contributors whether or not they were already on the staff, so my earnings grew, particularly when I was appointed by McCarthy to write a column every Saturday under the title 'Things you didn't know until now'—little snippets of useless information, which were finally killed by Sir Walter Layton, the chairman, but not before Tangye had, unknown to me, inserted a piece of pure invention about a centipede having ninety-nine legs. Tangye was at this time an ebullient amusing rogue. We went on holiday together to St Tropez where he behaved outrageously for that time, taking his clothes off and carrying a pretty girl with whom I thought I was in love into the sea. He also steered me into the local brothel, where we saw our first blue film. In London we shared a divided office with a thin partition between the halves. This nearly caused me a grave injury for Tangye picked up a rifle and bayonet, which I had hired as part of a costume with which to illustrate some piece of fiction, and plunged the bayonet through the wall just missing my shoulder; this was to him a great joke.

The leader page had an excellent team of writers, all of whom I got to know well because I handled their copy—A. J. Cummings, Vernon Bartlett, Hubert Philips, D. B. Wyndham Lewis and Robert Lynd. Wyndham Lewis's weekly column was called 'Beyond the Headlines' and required an illustration done at great speed, for which we found a young Polish artist, Felix Topolski, who would produce up to six sketches instead of one, so my right-hand bottom drawer gradually filled up with unused Topolskis, until he came in and asked to have them all back. Robert Lynd's essay appeared every Saturday. I had to go up to talk with him every Thursday, armed with suggestions to get him started. He would never start writing until he had shot my suggested subjects down. He kept a pile of half-crowns on his desk to give to beggars who called on him for help. Hubert Philips, who wrote under the name Dogberry, was the ugliest man imaginable, but a great talker and a great *homme à femmes*. We shared a secretary at one time, as we had adjacent offices, but he got the best of her. She was rather beautiful but not very bright and nearly landed me in serious trouble. I had had the silly idea of offering five pounds for the oldest family photograph; the next morning there were hundreds of letters which she had opened scattering photographs in all directions; the following morning there were thousands —I could not get into my office for mail bags; but the damage had been done, it took weeks to sort out, for almost nobody had identified his or her photograph and I had not demanded it.

Later on I had the opportunity of transferring the readers' letters to the leader page since a survey had shown that letters were very popular. I therefore sought letters from prominent people starting with one from a surgeon who had carried out an abortion on a girl who had been raped by a soldier in Hyde Park. At his trial he had been acquitted and explained in his letter why he had done it and why he would do it again. This had an immediate effect. Putting letters on the leader page trebled or quadrupled the number received and I was very pleased—until there was a telephone call from Birmingham from Mr Lawrence Cadbury, the proprietor, asking who was in charge of the letter column. He asked at what time I did them—five o'clock—and said that he would be in my office at five o'clock each day until the editor returned from holiday; then the letters were put back on their original page and the post bag returned to its normal size and anodyne content and peace reigned, though to be fair that was the only example in my experience of proprietorial interference by Mr Cadbury. I was, of course, at that time no longer assistant to the leader page editor. I had gone up a bit. The abdication crisis had blown up when Tangye Lean was in Egypt. McCarthy was ill and there was no one between me and the editor. The crisis was perfect feature material. We had to be ready for any eventuality. We commissioned all manner of articles. I worked night and day—literally. I got a camp bed installed in my office and slept there. Afterwards I had a bout of shingles, but I was promoted to leader page editor, Tangye becoming the book page editor on Robert Lynd's retirement, a job he had always wanted. We had made only one mistake. The Manchester edition had to have everything including pictures ready for printing exactly as in London. I was sending a constant stream of instructions up there, but, alas, I did not make clear the difference between photographs of Mrs Simpson and the Queen, so a first Manchester edition for the Outer Hebrides went to press welcoming our new queen with a picture of Mrs Simpson.

The *News Chronicle* was proud of its reputation as a left wing liberal organ. I learned the advantage of this reputation very early on when I was sent to Waterloo Station to interview Mr Herbert Morrison on his return from the United States. I did not have to interview him for on hearing the words *New Chronicle*, he volunteered to write an article for us, an offer I accepted. It was in fact interesting to see how many people of eminence were glad to be invited to write for us, the most eminent being, I suppose, George Bernard Shaw and H. G. Wells, the latter being rather difficult to deal with. It was not that he was unwilling but that he laid down very strict rules: so much a word, including '*a*' and '*the*'; a written agreement not to change anything, not even a comma; and an agreement not to cut anything—though to be truthful he seldom either over- or underwrote. Perhaps the most difficult author I commissioned was the painter Paul Nash. He asked to be allowed to do his own page layout to which I agreed, not knowing that he was going to have the whole article upside down. It was typical of Gerald Barry to allow it, though what Sir Walter Layton thought I do not know. Sir Walter was a very meticulous man who occasionally sat long over problems. I remember taking the proof of a leader about Anthony Eden's resignation for him to approve. He spent so long studying it that we nearly missed the edition; at last he made his mark; he put one word 'high' between 'his' and 'office'. On another occasion he said to me, 'Reilly, your otiose features will be the death of this newspaper.'

He was, though, very helpful to me when I put on display the results of weeks of private work. Robert Furneaux Jordan, the architect brother of Philip Jordan of the *News Chronicle*, Bernard King, the *News Chronicle* artist, and I borrowed the use of Sir Edwin Lutyens' studio in Mansfield Street in which to prepare a number of political posters which we would offer to any candidate MP who would oppose Neville Chamberlain and his government. The messages were very simple, 'Wrong about Manchuria, wrong about Ethiopia, wrong about Albania—and still they are in power, why?' supported by photographs of the guilty men. We produced about thirty of these posters and then borrowed the Grosvenor Place offices of the Gas Light and Coke Company from Sir Francis Goodenough in which to show them to all kinds of anti-government interests. Sir Walter Layton opened the exhibition for us. It created quite a lot of interest and elicited a promise from the Liberal Party of funds to pay for reproductions, but the war was coming and our minds were soon on other things. A few weeks passed before we returned to Mansfield Street, by which time Sir Edwin had burned all our work, which had overnight become seditious. Lady Emily Lutyens, our great ally, was as sad as we were.

Another political adventure was a visit which Michael Foot and I paid to the Albert Hall to attend one of Sir Oswald Mosley's rallies. The hall was packed and we could find space only in the topmost gallery but as we were on the main axis we had a very good view—not only of what was going on below but also of the violence above, for the blackshirts were busy ejecting objectors, picking them up by arms and legs and swinging them like sheep down the stairs. We held our peace until Mosley began to speak and uttered such foul rubbish that Michael exploded, whereupon we were set upon by half a dozen blackshirts who pinned us to our seats saying, 'You will hear the leader out and in silence.' The more I thought afterwards of that occasion the happier I was at the outcome of a dinner at the Hotel Curzon in Brighton where my father was staying at which Stafford Cripps said he would put an end to all political shirts by threatening to dress his young socialists in red; the police would then have to ban the wearing of uniforms. Cripps was in Brighton to speak at the Corn Exchange at my father's invitation. As there was no money for posters we resorted to chalk on the newly-laid pink surface along the front. My father, being rather too old to bend down, fixed his piece of chalk to the end of his umbrella. We had quite a good meeting nonetheless.

Gerald Barry, the editor of the *News Chronicle*, was passionately interested in architecture so I had little difficulty in persuading him to allow me to go with Barnett Saidman, the photographer, all over the country photographing and writing about buildings. The first time we did this we printed the pictures in date order, covering a century at a time. For the second year, at the request of the circulation manager, we published them county by county, but in both cases always on the Saturday back page. The third year we did types of building and thus built up a splendid collection of prints which, had the war not come, we intended to produce as a book. It would have been quite a good book for at that time I prided myself on being able to date any building to within twenty-five years and was getting round to being able to do the same for furniture and clothing. Saidman was one of three or four brothers all of whom were photographers, but Barnett was the best of them. He would spend hours waiting for the sun to get into the right position, or for a couple of swans, as at Moreton Old Hall, to do the same. The Moreton Old Hall picture was so good we gave it half the page and at the same time appealed successfully for funds to save the building. This series led to my becoming the staff writer on architecture and design and even to understudying Tangye Lean as deputy ballet critic, a post which led to my marrying a ballet dancer, Pamela Foster. The wedding ceremony took place in Caxton Hall one lunch time during the first week of the war. Michael Foot was my best man, a service I was to perform afterwards for him.

Journalism was a reserved occupation at the beginning of the war so I spent a year as features editor, Tangye Lean having joined the BBC and McCarthy having become editor of the *Star*. The editorial offices had by this time moved from the east to the west side of Bouverie Street so I had to give up my old Dickensian office—literally so, since he had been editor of the *Daily News*—and move into an open plan room shared by a large number of people, including Arthur Koestler just back from Spain. He shared my secretary and made better use of her than I did, but I was to write one more article. The American consul in Düsseldorf was the brother of one of my colleagues and over a drink at El Vino's he told me of a new symbol that was appearing on German factory walls. He then described the three arrows that I had sported in Germany. I sat down at once to write a piece advocating that we should fight the war with the three arrows as our symbol, that our aeroplanes should have them on their wings instead of the roundels. This produced two letters—one from Augustus John to the editor praising my suggestion to the skies, and the other from the authorities calling me up.

My last memories of the *News Chronicle* were of the Blitz. We took it in turns to roof-spot and had a button on the roof to ring a bell throughout the building with a code to describe the nearness of the danger. One night I just kept my finger on the button as a thing like a trunk hanging from a parachute slowly and silently drifted over the building. It destroyed a great deal of the Temple. Next morning I recovered a piece of the parachute from the Temple garden; and when I got home to Hampstead I found a long sliver of glass protruding from the plywood panelling immediately above my pillow. We had had our first bomb.

3

Wartime

'Go home,' 'You'll be sorry,' 'Turn round before it's too late.' With such expressions of welcome was I received at Perham Down into the 54th Training Regiment of the Royal Armoured Corps. I had not chosen to go into the army. My first choice had been the navy, but in October 1940 one did as one was told. I had stopped at Oxford on my way to camp to have my hair cut. I had asked for a proper military cut, so did not warm to the sergeant major who inspected us next morning and who called me two paces forward and then shouted at me, 'Who do you think you are? Bloody Mozart? Hair cut.' One other chap in the squad was also told to get his hair cut. He had the whole lot shaved off, so was duly 'jankered' for dumb insolence. We were a mixed bunch in age, size and background, but we all came from London. The previous week's intake had all come from Birmingham; they could not have been more helpful to the new boys, coming into our hut and showing us what to do.

I soon found in the camp two sympathetic characters who made life more bearable—Lawrence Whistler, the artist–craftsman brother of Rex Whistler the artist, and Humphrey Spender, the painter brother of Stephen Spender, the poet. Our sergeant was twenty-four years old and called Gorman. He got a commission, survived the war and emigrated to Australia. He telephoned me one day when I was lecturing in Sydney. He was a first-class soldier, whose keenness must have rubbed off on us, for when the day came for our passing out parade we marched onto the square and halted with such precision that Colonel Paul instantly passed us out and then asked us to show him some drill. We were all very proud of ourselves and of our sergeant. Colonel Paul was in the 11th Hussars, as indeed were almost all our officers. I came across him once when he sent for me to ask whether I knew anything about an unfriendly article about the army that had appeared in the *News Chronicle*. As I had written it, I had to confess. He said it was such a grave offence that I would have to go down to Tidworth to see the brigadier, who in turn tore strips off me. Two weeks later I faced the same brigadier at my OCTU board. 'I know Trooper Reilly,' he said, 'not officer material'—end of interview; and end of me, I thought, for I could not conceive of spending any longer in the ranks. As I left the room the regimental Adjutant, an elderly King's Royal Rifle Corps Major, told me not to worry. There were better regiments than the 11th Hussars. He said that I should try to get into either the 60th or the Rifle Brigade—'a much better lot to die with.' Fortunately that was not required of me, for I was shortly afterwards summoned by my squadron commander and shown a signal requiring Trooper Reilly to report to the Admiralty to see Admiral Godfrey, the Director of Naval Intelligence. It appeared that a member of the DNI's staff had recommended me, a Lieutenant Robert Harling, whom I used to commission to draw maps of sensitive areas of the world for the *News Chronicle*.

Admiral Godfrey explained that he wanted a journalist to go to Lisbon and report anything he could pick up, wearing civilian clothes. I jumped at it, had a second interview with the Deputy DNI, Colonel Lamplough, and a third with Commander Ian Fleming, to whom I was to report, and was assured that being the Senior Service they could get me out of the army; indeed I heard Colonel Lamplough telephone my camp to give them the good news. I returned to Salisbury Plain, as I thought to pack my bags, but that took six weeks—six weeks of agonised waiting. When at last my release came through and I reported to the Admiralty, I found that DNI had not been able to wait and had sent someone else to Lisbon. I consulted with Robert Harling who said leave it to him, go home and wait until he got in touch. So after a visit to Simpsons to get a sub-lieutenant's uniform with a green line for special branch on the sleeve, I spent four more weeks doing nothing —a useful time privately because we had moved to a garage cottage at Clewer, near Windsor, and my wife was expecting a baby. In due course I was ordered to Greenwich to be turned into a naval officer and then Robert Harling, as good as his word, told me that I was to join the Interservice Topographical Department (ISTD) and work at the Royal Patriotic Schools at Wandsworth interviewing escapists from Europe, since anyone arriving in Britain had to pass through Wandsworth for vetting by MI5, MI6, immigration officers and sundry other bodies. Apparently no one had told anyone there about me so I was not allowed in until MI5 had looked into me. I was sent home for another four weeks.

The job I was ultimately to do covered intelligence gathering of every kind from the strictly physical and topographical to colour pieces on morale, from orders of battle to political assessments, but concentrating towards the end on details of the Western Wall. It is difficult to evaluate this sort of work, particularly after so many years. Perhaps I may be allowed to quote from Donald McLachlan's book *Room 39 Naval Intelligence in Action 1939–45*:

'Back in London men from the typographical and newspaper world like Robert Harling, Paul Reilly and Hippisley-Coxe, all of them young Royal Naval Volunteer Reserve officers who combined in singular measure persuasive charm and ruthless vigour, were building up the sources of intelligence from contacts, refugees and business houses. Dull-sounding work, perhaps, but in the atmosphere of the early days exciting and exacting because of the feeling that the tide must soon turn and information was being built up as ammunition for future offensives.'

When I was eventually cleared I attached myself to a jolly MI9 Major Acton Burnell, who spoke excellent French and

German, and gradually we built up quite a reputation for the extensive detail contained in our Royal Patriotic Schools reports. The reports' circulation list got longer and longer until one day I was summoned to the Admiralty to face a furious DNI, who asked who on earth had given permission for one of his officers to be associated with such work. When I protested that it was tempting to extract the maximum of information from anyone coming at great risk from occupied Europe, but if he insisted I would confine myself to topographical questions, he calmed down and I was allowed to carry on. It was surprising how many escapists there were and with what regularity they came—weekly boats from Norway and at one time from Brittany. The Brittany boats were mostly organised by a M. Sibiril and came mainly from Morlaix. Eventually he himself had to escape and was a mine of information. I particularly liked the man from Quimper who arrived in a bowler hat and blue suit: 'I knew I was coming to London,' he said. I found it difficult to believe all I was told. A young Austrian, son of a general called von Haas, described to me in great detail the gas chambers and incinerators in a concentration camp; his job had been to clean the incinerators. A Dutchman described not only having worked as an Organisation Todt labourer on a flying bomb site, but also, more importantly, his spell at Peenemünde; his was one of the earliest accounts of the German V2 rocket and we knew of its importance by the number and grading of the brass that came down to interview him further. Another Dutchman was one day describing his escape to me with the help of a chart and, when I asked him to trace his course out of the Scheldt, I noticed his pencil going over some very shallow water. I asked him the draught of his boat when to my surprise he began to shake and got into such a muddle that I suggested MI5 should look at him again. This they did and he crossed the road to Wandsworth gaol, where I lost trace of him, though I think he was executed as a spy.

Admiral Godfrey rightly thought that all his officers should go to sea from time to time. When my turn came I was posted to

HMS *King George V* at Scapa Flow. I had never been in such an enormous vessel. It was alarming finding one's way afloat after a long slow railway journey and a short quick trip in a pinnace which ended in climbing on board and saluting the officer saluting me. I soon learned a frightening thing about the *King George V*; the commander of the ship had made a rule that every officer who joined should speak to the whole ship's company in the hangar on any subject of his choice. I knew that I could not do this and consulted the padre, who said that he would arrange for me to do it over a loud hailer in his cabin. I spoke about the French Resistance, drawing on my experience of interviewing escapists, and it went down rather well. It certainly led to a good deal of discussion in the ward room—a good deal of political discussion, against which I had been warned before leaving London. So when I was summoned by Captain Mack, and was greeted with, 'I hear you have been talking politics in the ward room,' I expected the worst. I did not expect to be asked up on the quarter deck to talk politics with the captain of the ship. My last meeting with Captain Mack, who was killed shortly afterwards in an air crash, was when he sent for me on my return from a flight in the *King George V*'s *Walrus*, to introduce me to the visiting captain of another battleship as an officer with plenty to say and plenty of guts—this because I had volunteered to be catapulted off the ship. The plenty to say was egged on by Lieutenant Robinson—later the Rt Hon. Sir Kenneth Robinson—who seemed to enjoy my presence in the ward room as much as I enjoyed his. My sea time was extended by two weeks in HMS *Havoc*, a destroyer, but from the point of view of the Royal Patriotic Schools my most useful time at sea was in the submarine HMS *Upright*, for I had to interview many foreign labourers who had worked in German yards. It was also the most scaring time for we spent forty-five minutes at the bottom of the North Sea. 'Oh Lord, another *Thetis*,' groaned a joker.

My last interrogation before going abroad was not at the Royal Patriotic Schools, but at a camp at Ealing which had been set up to take a large contingent of Russians who had been liberated at Cherbourg; they had all been working until a few weeks before D-Day for the Organisation Todt on the Channel Islands. As I do not speak Russian I had to send for help from the Admiralty who chose as my interpreter a Lieutenant Alec Penn, a former Russian who had spent most of the war as a liaison officer in a Russian submarine. After the war he made a fortune selling all kinds of metal shop fittings to Marks and Spencer. The commandant of the camp had found one Russian who had some German and had therefore nominated him to be the camp leader. When we arrived we found a surprising lack of goodwill—indeed a complete refusal by everyone to give us any information. Penn then had the good idea, which won the camp commandant's approval, that the Russians should be invited to choose their own camp leader by the following morning. When we turned up next morning we found them all queueing up to answer our questions and, even more surprising, we found that they had elected the same man as our camp commandant had appointed to be their leader—a good example of canteen democracy in action. By the time we had seen them all we must have pin-pointed every bunker and machine gun post on every island—a mass of useless information, since it was decided not to invade.

Since I was still on the strength of the Inter-Service Topographical Department or Naval Intelligence Division 21, they had the right to send me where they wished and they wished Paris, which had just fallen. My remit was to collect all information I could about French Indochina. I was attached to an American unit, a branch of the Office of Strategic Services, doing a similar job with an office in the Avenue Kleber. I was billeted in the British Officers' Transit Camp, the Hotel de l'Arcade. I was clearly quite a mystery to the French for I soon found myself being courted by various senior French officers and being invited to their headquarters in the Hotel Continentale. I even had a meeting with Colonel de Vavrin, head of de Gaulle's Bureau Central de Renseignements et

10. With Lord Snowdon in a Czechoslovakian glass factory

11. HM The Queen Mother in The Design Centre

12. Talking with HRH The Princess Margaret

d'Action, which made me feel that I should be reporting these contacts to DNI who was by this time Admiral Rushbrooke, my step-father-in-law. He sent me to Broadway where I saw a Commander RN in MI6, who said the French obviously thought I was working for the Intelligence Service, or l'IS. (they had lost the TD) and were trying to find out what I was interested in. I was told to go back and remember every question I was asked, for their questions, it seemed, would be of considerable interest to our intelligence service. But the French soon discovered that I was working for a topographical department and lost all interest in me.

I, however, was much enjoying being in Paris. I had a Peugeot 410 lifted from the Germans, until I lent it to an American colleague who told me that it had been stolen from him; he was so flush thereafter that I was sure he had flogged it. I had scored a minor success at a gathering of French businessmen who had just been addressed in English by an OSS colonel, by talking to them in French; I had by then also added to my team a French Commandant de Vaisseau, seconded by their *Deuxième Bureau*, whose great ambition was to get to Oxford where my headquarters were. He acted as a courier, taking and returning all the railway profiles, town plans, maps, etc. which we had extracted from their owners. There was an arrangement whereby everything that we shipped to Oxford would be copied for the Americans, but whether the reverse applied I am not sure—though at least as far as I know they made no charge for my use of their office.

I went as often as possible to the British Officers' Club in the Rue St Honoré where one could eat and drink and dance. One evening I saw at the far end of the ballroom Margot Fonteyn in ENSA uniform. Remembering that she and my wife were friends I went over to ask her to dance. She agreed as the band struck up a Viennese waltz. Undeterred I took the plunge and Margot and I sailed out onto the vast expanse of the floor—but nobody followed us. Thus I could—and still can—claim to have danced a solo with the greatest ballerina of her day. We made a date to buy my wife some French underwear next morning—a hilarious expedition with Margot modelling and me haggling. There was another nice club in the Avenue de Friedland, run I think by the British Embassy, where I used to have lunch. It was there that I took a pre-war girlfriend whom I met again in the course of duty. I had first met and fallen for her in 1937 at St Tropez, where I was on holiday with Tangye Lean—a holiday memorable for my having fished a gravely injured Le Corbusier from under the keel of a speed boat; when I telephoned the news to the *News Chronicle* my editor said, 'Sit by his bedside and get his story,' which I did, but as he did not die there was no story. Her parents had a large house behind Tahiti Plage; one of her uncles was a newspaper proprietor. She was very beautiful, but very conservative. At the time of Munich she defended our appeasement, so I wrote her off. As part of my work in Paris I had to talk with a shipping magnate who asked me back to his flat to meet his wife. It was she. She had not changed very much.

Another friend of mine, who had also seemed to survive the war without too much pain, gave me an introduction to the boss of the Cirque Medrano who wanted nothing so much as English pound notes for which he would pay well over the odds. I had a friend in Naval Intelligence Division, Anthony Hippisley-Coxe, who was a real aficionado of the circus—in fact at one time he had been a professional, having trained and presented a troupe of performing cats—so we had to find an excuse for him to visit Paris. Medrano received him with enthusiasm.

My life in Paris was made easier for me by the presence of my cousin, Patrick Reilly, who had recently arrived from North Africa with Duff Cooper. One of the perks of his office was access to a regular motor torpedo boat to Newhaven. He promised to get me home for Christmas, but as luck would have it I caught a bad attack of flu. I went nonetheless and stood on the bridge for the whole journey across the Channel. By the time we reached Newhaven the flu had disappeared.

After Christmas the reverse happened. The flu returned as soon as I stepped ashore at Dieppe. This trip coincided with the German Ardennes offensive which had the effect of disbanding the OSS unit to which I was attached in Paris. My American colleagues seemed to lose their nerve. They packed up and fled, leaving themselves hardly time to say good bye.

But my own time in Paris was coming to an end. When I reported to my headquarters in Oxford, they were talking about the Dutch East Indies rather than French Indochina; their clients, Combined Operations, were pressing ISTD for all they could unearth; ISTD had to have someone in Holland to do the digging; I was the person chosen. So I went to Brussels to seek the views of Admiral Dickens, who was to be Naval Officer in Command in The Hague. He said that there were several different ways of getting into Holland: parachute, night landing from a submarine or with the army. I chose the army. I first needed to draw my khaki battledress and revolver etc. from the dockyard at Chatham, then to join the Dutch Lieutenant Commander Bink and his handful of marines and to pick up my own marines and their transport, and thus to cross the Channel as an Anglo-Dutch Target Force. Our first stop was at Venlo where once more Lieutenant Commander Harling looked after us by attaching our small party to his Royal Marine Commando, thereby enabling us to eat well and sleep in a commandeered convent. Then into Germany crossing the Rhine by a Bailey bridge at Xanten and seeing our first sight of actual war—the flattened and still burning towns of Cleve and Emmerich and in the fields between hundreds of our gliders all now empty. After reporting to Supreme Headquarters Allied Expeditionary Force headquarters we were attached to the Canadian Army and, being an independent unit, we drove back into Holland to overtake the troops, finding our way as best we could. We went by Nijmegen, Arnhem, where the bushes still carried commando berets and the fields the swollen, stinking carcasses of dead cattle, and on up to Groningen where we saw for the first time a group of women with shaven heads—the price of collaboration—and our first Canadian soldiers. Our first target was in Groningen, a library full of information about the Dutch East Indies, so we began to fill our spare vehicles and then pressed on across the north of Holland, stopping on the way for lunch with Bink's farming family. They gave us all they could spare which was potatoes and potatoes and potatoes, three courses of them each cooked differently. This had been their diet for a long time, but at least they had plenty, unlike those who lived in the cities.

And so to Leeuwarden and Deventer and then to Wageningen where we had to stop since the front line went through the middle of that small town. The commanding officer at the British headquarters, once over his surprise at seeing my naval shoulder tabs and naval cap, wrapped as it was in khaki, pointed out on his town plan our two local targets, but warned us to take care crossing a road which the Germans had under fire. As I was in command of our little target force I decided to cross first and got across safely. I then had to wait and watch until we were all over and have since wondered whether I did the right thing to go first, though the Germans were asleep that afternoon and did not fire.

It was in Wageningen that I came across an aspect of the German military that I found sickening, namely the way they defecated everywhere, in the beds, on the sofas, in the armchairs, on the carpets. On VE Day we drove as fast as we could westwards towards Utrecht and being an independent unit we got there first. We were received like conquering heroes and were carried shoulder high into the Hotel des Pays Bas and given the best rooms, for an hour or so only, for when the real troops arrived the CO ousted us and we spent that night in the stables. But two memories will stay with me—first the pleasure and indeed surprise to be saluted wherever we went by fully armed German soldiers, and second the sight of starving Dutch folk sitting on the pavements, too weak and emaciated to stand up. The Germans had deliberately prevented any food from being delivered to the main Dutch towns for the last months of the war—an act of unbelievable cruelty for which they will not be forgiven.

Our main target was, of course, The Hague whither we sped on the morrow. It was a busy city, full of Canadians making love quite openly to willing Dutch girls. Bink and I found ourselves rooms in the Hotel de Wittebrug, the Anglo–Dutch naval mess, and set about calling on people with knowledge of the Dutch East Indies. The Dutch knew much more about their Asian empire than the French did about theirs and we soon needed extra hands to help. I thought for a moment that I had found some extra transport for I discovered in a naval barracks a magnificent convertible Horch, with great exhausts coming out of the bonnet: I proudly drove it back to the hotel, but had to hand it over to the chief of staff who said, 'Thank you very much. Just what I wanted.' There were in those same barracks two V2s which had not been fired. Our best find was a great cache of *Marketenderväre*—spirits of all kinds—in a bunker near Scheveningen. This kept our mess afloat free of charge for weeks. Rather sadder was a special bottle that two Dutch people opened for us. Speaking perfect English they asked us into their house and showed us their prize bottle of Napoleonic Esterhazy Tokay. We begged them not to open it but they said there would never again be such an occasion, so they duly broke the seal, took the cork out and poured a dirty brown undrinkable liquid. A better drink was offered us by a party of Americans, members of OSS, who had been in The Hague for six months wearing civilian clothes.

The work we were doing was very satisfactory, involving plenty of travel, sightseeing and meeting people from the highest to the lowest. I had a long conversation one day with Dr Schermerhorn, the Dutch Prime Minister, who particularly wanted to know what was going to be the result of our 1945 election. When I told him that Labour was going to win, he would not believe it. When Labour did win, he asked me back to try to find out how I knew. Another more lasting friendship grew out of my admiration for the Van Nelle factory in

Rotterdam. I had tried to visit it before the war, for it was the most modern factory I had ever seen, but they would not let me in. There was no problem in 1945. I was taken in to meet the chairman, Kees van der Leeuw, who turned out to be a very unusual man. He spent his mornings as a psychiatrist in Amsterdam—he had been trained in Vienna—and his afternoons in Rotterdam as a manufacturer of tea and coffee. Later he became Chairman of the trustees of the Kröller Muller Museum at Otterlo and Chairman of the Delft Technical University. We became close friends. My second wife and I went over to see him in Wassenaar on the day of his death. We telephoned but he did not answer.

My last mission in uniform was also for the ISTD but this time I was travelling under the Prime Minister's orders; everyone was invited to help Lieutenant Commander Reilly, who set off from Paris for Vienna on the first post-war Orient Express. It was a very slow journey. At one point the train came to so long a halt that I got up to see what was wrong. We were standing in the station of Enns just as I had got to the crossing of the Enns in my *War and Peace*. I did not read it again until my return journey. My mission was to bring back from St Lambrecht the vast collection of Eastern European topographical information without any of it falling into Russian hands—a rather strange instruction since Mr Ernest Bevin had just made his well-publicised speech about putting his cards on the table face upwards. The collection was stored in the library of the monastry at St Lambrecht. Nearby in the church, behind a false wall, was one of the main German collections of pornography, about which news travelled very fast to Vienna, attracting all manner of top brass who would come down ostensibly to see the topographical library but actually to see and steal the pornography. The method I chose for shipping the topographical collection back to London was not by sea from Trieste, though that would have been possible, not by air because that would have trailed the collection under too many noses, but by train, for there was a daily leave train from Villach to Calais. The train, however, could take only one carload at a time, so it took a week to get the whole lot to the coast. I had managed to assemble a good supply of NAAFI spirit rations, including the Christmas 1945 quota, and had packed my personal loot into the train; from Calais I managed to signal this fact to Dover and thus was fetched with my bottles in a naval vehicle and swept out of the port area without any customs. I got home the day before my demobilisation.

4

America

Throughout the war the *News Chronicle* had been paying me a small supplement, not enough to make up my pay, but enough to make me feel that I would be welcomed back after the war. I was hoping to be given a political column to write, for throughout my service I had been preparing myself, first at the Royal Patriotic Schools, thereafter in France and Holland. But the newspaper was only four pages thick after the war; it had been thirty or thirty-two pages before. Gerald Barry said there was no job for me but, if I could get another one elsewhere, he would not try to get from me any of the money the paper had been paying me. So I was jobless until, at Robert Harling's suggestion, I applied for the editorship of a magazine on the plastics industry. I was interviewed by Theo Stephens, a director of Newnes and Pearsons, who confessed to as little knowledge of plastics as I had, but who said it should be easier to turn a journalist into a chemist than a chemist into a journalist, and anyway they intended to send their man to New York to work on the American magazine *Modern Plastics*. I got the job and, after a while going round the main British plastic firms, I sailed in SS *Port Huon* for my first trip to New York. On board I met William McMillan, being sent across to open a New York office for the *Manchester Guardian*; we became and remained great friends.

The *Port Huon* was a cattle ship with space for about twelve passengers. She travelled very slowly, taking fifteen days to cross, but we passed through every kind of weather from the very rough to a foggy mill pond. I had been booked an apartment in West 103rd Street on the eighteenth floor. 'Have a good trip, Paul,' said my taxi driver as he helped me with my luggage. 'How do you know my name?' I asked. 'It's on your bag, isn't it?' he replied. Half an hour later I went to post a card. I could not see a post box in the post office so I asked a chap standing there where I should put the card. 'How the hell should I know?' he replied. Next morning at breakfast I made another mistake. I said 'Thank you.' 'What's that you said?' 'I said thank you.' 'Don't waste my time.' New York takes some getting used to, but try as I might I could not get used to the cockroaches which traipsed across the bare boards of my apartment all night, rattling like dried leaves. I had to move and eventually found a brownstone house in East 53rd Street which I shared with the McMillans.

Modern Plastics at that time was one of a stable of four publications—two magazines and two catalogues—all owned by Charles Breskin who ruled his one floor of Chanin Building in 42nd Street like an oriental potentate. What really gave him his authority was his complete control of the annual bonuses that he distributed at Christmas. Since these came to comfortable sums there was a great deal of manoevring and jockeying towards the end of the year with everyone trying to keep on his right side. I was glad not to be involved in these office politics, but I did owe him a great deal, for he knew everything in the American plastics industry and gave me innumerable introductions. Moreover he sent me all over the United States calling on factories and writing features for his magazine. He also encouraged me to pursue my own interests and to call upon the great names of American industrial design—people like Walter Dorwin Teague, Raymond Loewy and Henry Dreyfuss, who all became good friends. Another friend whom I was glad to meet again—we had first met at Oxford—was David Ogilvy, just beginning his fabulous career in advertising. He had a farm in Lancaster County, Pennsylvania in the middle of the Amish country where I spent a short holiday and was lucky enough to coincide with an Amish Sunday morning service in the great tobacco barn belonging to Ira Stolzfuss, a local tribal chief. It could not have been more interesting to watch the buggies driving up from early in the morning and unloading their black-coated, black-hatted, bearded but not mustachio'd men, and full-skirted, white-aproned women; to sit with the men facing the women in the barn; to listen to the singing without any musical instruments and to detect in what was sung Roman Catholic chants coming from Anabaptist throats; and to witness in the middle of the twentieth century so many survivals of the seventeenth.

Half way through my time in New York I was suddenly asked by Theo Stephens in London to try to sell *Chambers Encyclopaedia* which Newnes and Pearson had bought. They had come to an arrangement with the publisher of an American encyclopaedia who had agreed to test the market. I was asked to work with him. We decided to sample the taste of Brooklyn for encyclopaedias, he taking one side of the street, I the other. We planned to use the old subterfuge of pretending to be pollsters seeking information about the standards of education and found it worked well—at least it opened doors and allowed us to get a foot in. Wherever we found an encyclopaedia already installed we knew our chances to be good for we would be simply pandering to an addiction. After a week I was able to tell London that Chambers would have a future in the USA.

A regular weekly chore was one which I undertook voluntarily and which won me some following in the British plastics industry. I suggested to my London employers that if I were to write a weekly letter they should reproduce it and distribute it to all main companies in the industry, free of charge, as a sort of advance publicity for the editor of their proposed magazine. America was greatly in advance of Britain in plastics technology so it was not difficult for a journalist to pick up things that were new. In those days plastics which are today household words, like acrylic and vinyl, were spelled out at their chemical length, such as polymethylmethacrilate and polyvinylchloride while what is today known as Teflon was then just on the American market as polytetrafluoroethylene; everyone knew it had a great future but no one could say what. The excitement in America in those days was that the chemists were constantly writing formulae for new plastics and constantly predicting their properties, but sadly the market produced the most awful trash. There were of course exceptions. The firm Rohm and Haas spent much time and money on its design policy, producing excellent models for fabricators to copy in the company's Plexiglas, while other companies employed industrial design consultants and yet others claimed to do so without having met one. There was a practice at that time of making up names of designers and applying them to products, for it sounded right to have a designer, at least it did in America. But whether in America or Britain, in those days plastic mouldings came in the crudest colours such as are to be found today only wherever standards of living are low—in places like Portugal, Spain or Yugoslavia, Bulgaria or the Soviet Union.

I recall two companies in England which tried to set standards—ICI and Runcolite Ltd; ICI plastics division was at that time under the chairmanship of Dr Walter Worboys who commissioned various designers such as Peter Lambda to produce models to be made in Perspex (he later became Chairman of the Council of Industrial Design); and Runcolite Ltd run by William Fischbein, who commissioned Mrs Gaby Schreiber to design all manner of small domestic products like cups and saucers, tumblers and sugar bowls (they later got married and lived in a beautiful house in Sussex where they gave magnificent parties). She eventually moved her office to Chelsea, where it was opened by the Duke of Edinburgh, Mr Heath being among the favoured guests. My main contribution to the British plastics industry was to speak highly to De La Rue about Formica, which they subsequently bought and as a result they put me on their great annual dinner list for the next thirty years. My London link man was Walter Williams, editorial director of the National Trade Press (as my employers had become), who encouraged me by reporting the reception of my letters and who eventually supported my request to travel back for Christmas 1946 first class in the *Queen Elizabeth 1*. Before embarking on the most influential journey of my life, I was stood a farewell lunch at the Waldorf Astoria by Charles Breskin for the senior members of his staff at the end of which he made a generous speech about me to which, to my eternal shame, I was totally unable to reply; I was still completely tongue-tied and went through agonies of embarrassment and remorse during lunch and afterwards.

My farewell party aboard the *QE1* was much easier—no speeches and lots to drink. I must have had second sight when I asked permission to come back first class for I found myself at table with the Hon. Josiah Wedgwood and Mr (later Sir) Gordon Russell, both of them members of the newly founded Council of Industrial Design and both very willing to talk about the problems facing it. I was very willing to talk about my own experiences in America, about American industry and American designers; and I must have impressed Gordon Russell for when a year later he was appointed Director of the Council of Industrial Design he asked me to join him as head of his information division. But meanwhile I had to go back to the National Trade Press which was still intending to produce a magazine on the plastics industry, though they could not get started not having a paper ration—or rather only a ration for books. They set me to work producing a catalogue, like the one in America but with a staff of three instead of the dozen or so in New York, for a catalogue counted as a book. I returned to the United States in May 1947 to attend a convention of the American industry in Chicago accompanied by Charles Breskin who took me to some of the bluer joints in the city. I returned within the week in an old Constellation that had to feather two of its engines and come down in a hurry at Shannon.

When Gordon Russell asked me to join the Council of Industrial Design I had to get out of my contract with the National Trade Press and might not have achieved this had not the NTP bought the Temple Press magazines among which they found one on plastics and so did not need to start another one. When I broke my news to Charles Breskin—that I was joining the Council as a public relations officer—he could not believe it, for he recalled my inability to reply to him at his farewell lunch; but he wished me well. And so did my father, who died a month before I joined Gordon Russell; he urged me to get a good box of slides together and stick to it. Before finally accepting the COID's offer, I decided to ask the opinion of Sir Philip Hendy, the Director of the National Gallery. He said, 'If you can wear being called "public pansy No 1" certainly accept.' I could and did and joined on April Fools' Day 1948; and thus I found myself doing what came naturally, since design, together with politics, had always been my first love.

5

COID/Design Council

Alan Jarvis, the man I succeeded at COID, was a great friend of Stafford Cripps and under his influence left the Council to take part in the film world. He had an immense circle of friends and was a very good public speaker. He was also quite a good sculptor and did my head with moderate success. He ended his life in Canada, his last job being the directorship of the Canadian National Gallery. He was, though, exceedingly helpful to me and very clear in explaining the role ahead of me, which would obviously involve a lot of public speaking. I consulted an advertising-agent friend, who said, 'Come with me to the London Publicity Club—no need for you to say anything,' so we went along to Prince Harry's room in Fleet Street one evening and found about sixty people waiting for their teacher. He came in saying that this evening would be guest night; were there any guests? Hands up please; so up went mine, most reluctantly. I was beckoned forward, handed a slip of paper and asked to speak on that subject for three minutes. On the paper was one word 'emancipation'. I stood silently. He said, 'Start with "Ladies and Gentlemen;" so I said, 'Ladies and Gentlemen', and stopped. He said, 'You are obviously a drier up—not to worry, but try again;' 'Ladies and Gentlemen', and silence. 'Right; say, "Ladies and Gentlemen" and go on saying it until I tell you to stop.' This I did for about three minutes and then crept back into my seat, but the ice was broken or nearly so; at least I had learned the sound of my own voice. I have, though, never been an easy speaker, never an extempore one. I have always written everything down—or at least the first and last sentences. I was once so impressed by an after dinner speech by Lord Mancroft that I asked him if he had any tips that he would pass on to my colleagues at COID. We found an evening when he could do this and to my delight he came in with a fistful of papers and started by saying, 'Never ever get up to speak without notes in your hand, for even the best, most experienced speaker will occasionally dry up.' If that were not enough to convince, I just think of the opening of the Design Centre in the presence of Prince Philip, Mr Peter Thornycroft, the President of the Board of Trade and a full house, when our chairman, Sir Walter Worboys, tried to manage without his notes; half way through his speech he dried up; with panic on his face he fought to remember; he finally had to seek his script, but he could not recall into which pocket he had put it.

Gordon Russell could not have been kinder or more understanding about my private life which at this time was undergoing a dramatic change. My first marriage had been breaking up for several years when I met a young woman who had applied to the COID for a job. Bob Little, our textile specialist, wanted to take her on and asked me to see her. This I did, but she was never employed by the Council, for in those days we took on only graduates. When I sent for our personnel department's report on her I was amused to read that she was 'the honey-pot type.' We were married on 25 September, 1952.

I was very fortunate in the timing of my directorship of the Design Council, indeed of my twenty-nine years with the organisation. When I arrived in 1948 design was at its lowest ebb, but the public was ready, at least in patches. This had been proved in 1946 and 47 when people queued in their thousands to see the exhibition staged by the COID at the Victoria and Albert Museum called 'Britain Can Make It', around which were embroidered many variations such as 'Britain Can't Have It'. Of course that was true up to a point for the excellent things shown at the V & A were not, so soon after the war, readily available in the shops, though even had they been it is doubtful whether the shop-keepers would have taken any notice since the nigger in the wood-pile of design was, and still is, the retailer. In those early post-war days the difference between good and bad was so clear that a new word gained currency to describe the good, particularly in furniture, and that was 'contemporary'. This soon lent itself to 'contemptible' to the unfriendly; but it was never a satisfactory word for even journalists got confused by it. One of them once asked me which of six chairs was the most contemporary; I said I had left my stopwatch at home. To those who worked in the COID, however, it became a useful sort of shorthand; we all knew what we meant by it—we meant simplicity rather than complexity, good use of sensible materials, good workmanship and good appearance.

In those days there were two or three shops in London where one could count on finding good contemporary design —Bowman's of Camden Town, Heal's of Tottenham Court Road and Dunn's of Bromley, Anthony Heal and Geoffrey Dunn being real proseletisers, ready to go anywhere to spread the message. Both became valuable members of council of the COID and both good friends of mine. Geoffrey Dunn maintained his work for the Council as a judge or member of a committee or member of the Council itself from 'Britain Can Make It' right through to my retirement and even, I believe, thereafter. Anthony Heal wisely disposed of his shop to Terence Conran of Habitat/Mothercare who produced a miraculous transformation of the Heal's Building, after a very poor performance by a young man from the wrong end of the furniture industry, who had been brought in as a commercial wizard. He was typical, really, of the sort of person who did most damage to what the Design Council stood for. He had no sympathy for, nor understanding of contemporary design and thus turned Heal's into a poor version of Harrods. How sad, though, that commercial design could not also be good. How sad it was to hear arguments at the Council by people who should have known better, by people like John T. Murray and Colin King, for compromise in our selections. It always

13. With Michael Foot

14. With Sir John Betjeman

15. With Harold Wilson, when he was Prime Minister

16. With my predecessor, Sir Gordon Russell

seemed nonsense to me to argue for run of the mill commercial designs, when one was in receipt of public money to put the case for something better.

This argument is still going on, for the Design Council, after my retirement, set up a committee under David Mellor's chairmanship to examine the role of design in consumer goods and to my astonishment there were voices round that table speaking up for traditional design. I had, of course, once tried out the strength of traditional design, in the Design Centre when I asked Geoffrey Bemrose, the historian of pottery and the most knowledgeable figure in North Staffordshire, if he would choose those patterns which were still in production unaltered since their inception. This he was glad to do and assembled around twenty examples which we displayed with an explanation about their being still in production because they were in their day the best examples of contemporary design. But people did not understand that and only wondered why on earth the Design Council was exposing the past when its main objective was to stimulate present-day thinking. I was quite happy at that reaction for I was never in favour of retrospection, not even to make a point on behalf of contemporary work, because I shared Philip Rosenthal's conviction that design is a creative activity having nothing to do with reproduction, and I agreed with the nineteenth-century writer, Lewis F. Day, when he said, 'If we rely on copyism our failure is inevitable.' I used to like Geoffrey Dunn's call at our Design Index selection meetings for some contribution in every product that we were to accept. I was also glad to find support for my point of view in various nineteenth-century writings, particularly those relating to the Great Exhibition of 1851. In those I also found some admirable definitions of good design such as the regret expressed by the 1851 furniture jury, 'that there have not been more specimens of ordinary furniture for general use; works whose merits consist in correct proportion, simple but well considered design, beauty of material and perfect workmanship.' Or, though we might express Matthew Digby Wyatt's advice to designers rather less pretentiously today, we could hardly quarrel with his sentiments when he said:

'The highest property of design is that it speaks the universal language of nature which all can read. If, therefore, men be found systematically to deceive: by too direct an imitation of nature; by using one material in the peculiar style of conventionality universally recognised as incident to another; by borrowing ornaments expressive of lofty associations and applying them to mean objects; by hiding the structural purpose of the article and sanctioning, by a borrowed form, the presumption that it may have been made for a totally different object or in a perfectly different way – such men cannot clear themselves from the charge of degrading art by systematic misrepresentation.'

Owen Jones's most useful contribution to these discussions was his clear picture of that same vicious circle in industrial design which is still exercising our present-day propagandists. In a review of the Crystal Palace exhibits he said:

'Were we to enquire of the artists who designed these melancholy productions why they had chosen that particular form, they would undoubtedly tell us that those were the only styles of design which manufacturers would purchase; were we to enquire of the manufacturers why they had engaged in production of articles of so little worth, they would undoubtedly tell us that they were the only articles they could sell; were we to enquire of the public how it came to pass that they purchased such vile productions and admitted them to their homes to enfeeble their own taste and effectually to destroy that of their children, they would infallibly reply that they had looked everywhere for better things, but could not find them; so the vicious circle is complete.'

Ruskin, of course, was quite intolerant of this sort of buck-passing. Lecturing a few years later to an audience of Bradford art students he flatly asserted that, 'it rests with the manufacturer in any business to determine whether he will make his wares educational instruments or mere drugs of the market.'

These problems are still with us. As Sir Hugh Casson once said, 'We are thought to be a country that cares about modern things even if we have no modern things worth caring about.' He was of course right, as was Gladstone when he wrote in 1862, 'Teach the English people to love beauty; therein is their greatest need; if you do that you will have done what no politician can do or ever has done; and there can be no higher mission to perform than that.' I have always felt that our fault lies in our love of things past. Too many people and too many organs of opinion cast backward glances, finding merit in many aspects of Victorian design which the leading nineteenth-century critics deplored. Roger Fry warned against this when he wrote in 1919:

'And now having watched the whatnot disappear I have the privilege of watching its resurrection. I have passed from disgust, through total forgetfulness into the joys of retrospection. It is evident that we have just arrived at the point where our ignorance of life in the Victorian period is such as to allow the incurable optimism of memory to build a quite peculiar little earthly paradise out of the boredoms, the snobberies, the cruel repressions, the mean calculations and rapacious speculations of the mid-nineteenth century.'

And of course it is not only Victoriana that appeals; we go ferreting backwards through the centuries so that the great German pundit on things English, Dr Wilhelm Dibelius, could write in the 1930s of Britain, 'that nowhere else have the forms of the past so tenacious a hold upon the present.'

But the wheel of fashion never stands still. By 1967 I was writing in the *Architectural Review* an article called 'The Challenge of Pop' because it was clear to me that the Design

Council was somehow out of step with the young movements of the day. As Fiona McCarthy wrote in her excellent book *All Things Bright and Beautiful*, 'the Council seemed much closer to the world of Ambrose Heal than Terence Conran. It looked out of touch with swinging London; its zing and zest was minimal; it seemed almost out of date.' I said in my article that ten years earlier it had all been much easier; selectors armed with yardsticks of Bauhaus and Werkbund origins, with standards of functional efficiency, fitness for purpose, truth to materials and economy of means, had easily picked out sound design from meretricious.

'There was still in those days a consensus of informed, professional opinion in favour of direct, simple, unostentatious, almost neutral solutions . . . At the same time modern design became its own worst enemy through the very narrowness of choice offered . . . At this point the Design Centre, which had until then spearheaded the campaign against feeble imitations in favour of modern common sense, came into real danger of being hoist with its own petard.'

However I pointed out that the Design Centre had become unashamedly adventurous and obviously much influenced by, if not itself the initiator of, current trends, and that one reason for this change was the appointment of Barry Mazur to design the Centre's exhibitions. So I was able to finish my *Architectural Review* article with a renewed call for function and common sense. 'The need,' I said, 'is still to hold fast to quality, whether of thought or material or structure,' and I still believe that. And I still, like Thomas Carlyle, fight very shy of 'the collective wisdom of the individually ignorant'.

My first year with the Council of Industrial Design was partly spent in organising Design Weeks in various provincial cities like Cardiff, Manchester and Sheffield, each week being inaugurated by some VIP like Dr Hugh Dalton at Cardiff or Princess Margaret at Sheffield. A Design Week consisted of an exhibition called 'Design Fair' plus as many public meetings as could be fitted in. At Cardiff we had an excellent meeting for members of the Women's Institutes which was addressed by Mrs Alison Settle, who said that she begged God to preserve her from the tyranny of the three piece suite, a point of view that was cheered to the echo. When I retired from the Council twenty-nine years later the tyranny was still as intact as ever. It was in Manchester that I first had to open my mouth in public—an alarming occasion because it was in the presence of Dennis Clive, a colleague who was both junior to me and completely at home on his feet. He was the official organiser of our Design Weeks but, as Gordon Russell used to say, he would have been just as happy organising a herring week.

Another achievement of that first year was the launching of the magazine *Design*. I can take some credit for that, because although Alec Davis was editor, I was his chief and as head of the information division I had the main responsibility; and as a pre-war journalist I was the leader writer. The first issue appeared in January 1949 with a cover and logo by Robert Harling. The title of the magazine, the one word 'Design', was the suggestion of Robin Darwin, at that time a member of the Council. It has been the only consistent thing about the publication, which has oscillated fairly violently ever since. In the early years we chopped and changed our logos and covers until we settled on the logo done for us by Ken Garland. Before him we used Stuart Rose, F. H. K. Henrion and Peter Hatch, the last as our first in-house art editor. When *Design* was first published there was already on the market a private enterprise publication called *Art and Industry* which had an outspoken champion in Sir Francis Meynell who was a member of the Council. He argued forcefully against our launching out in competition, calling our intention empire building and ultimately resigning when we went ahead. I was comforted to receive at the end of March 1950 a letter from Meynell which read:

'You know how strongly critical I felt (and indeed still feel) about our publication of *Design*. The first few numbers gave me new reason for criticism—I did not think that a good job was being done. Now I want to say how good I think the new issue is—interesting in its contents, clear in its presentation.

'The muddled current form of *Art and Industry* is, I think, in part at least an unexpected, sad result of the publication of *Design*: an effort to jazz it up to be different. If only you had used the Council's taste, technique and resources to improve the already existing magazine . . .

'But I don't want to end on my grievance note. You have had enough of that! So let the last word be congratulations on a first rate number.'

The first year of *Design* was the excuse for the first of the innumerable little notes that I received from Gordon Russell throughout the twelve years for which I worked for him, all written in his marvellously clear handwriting and all phrased to enchant their recipient. The first one read, 'At the end of *Design*'s first year I write to its competent midwife to say how well I think the child is coming on. As you know I have always believed in it and in the early days had a good deal of criticism both inside and outside the Council which I didn't pass on as I felt so much of it was not constructive.'

For me personally there was a small gratification in being able to get *Design* started, for the country was still suffering from the paper rationing that had prevented my publishing a new magazine on plastics. It was, though, possible for me to publish our new magazine on design because, as a government sponsored body, the COID could draw on HMSO paper stocks —indeed HMSO was in fact the publisher in exchange for a substantial handling charge. Later this handling charge was to become a minor issue between the two institutions but one which was eventually sorted out in good humour with an exhibition of the work of HMSO being staged in the Design Centre. But that was a long way ahead; meanwhile the Council of Industrial Design found itself deeply involved with preparations for the 1951 Festival of Britain, an event which led to the COID taking on a great number of temporary staff in its industrial division under the leadership of Mark Hartland Thomas, who was the initiator of the 1951 Stock List. This was later to become the 1951 Design Review and afterwards, at the suggestion of a leader in *The Times*, Design Index, as it remained until 1981, when it became, for some reason, the Design Centre Selection. This piece of machinery was and remained the corner stone of the Council's activity, for it distinguished the Council's choice from the run of the mill; it was also the yardstick by which we were judged.

So much has been written about the Festival of Britain that I shall limit myself to the effects on me—to the exhilaration I felt on my every visit to the South Bank, particularly to F. H. K. Henrion's agriculture pavilion, indeed to any of the official Festival Exhibitions, especially perhaps to the one staged in Edinburgh by Wyndham Goodden; to the sense it made of my own job at the Council of Industrial Design, because it drew a clear line between commercial taste and designers' taste; to the pleasure I got from meeting and mixing with the host of architects and designers involved, most of whom became my lifelong friends; and to the opportunity of giving my first lecture at the Royal Society of Arts. This last was perhaps the most important for me personally and professionally—personally because I could never have imagined myself doing such a thing and being given a silver medal by the RSA for having done it; and professionally because having read enormously for it beforehand I was able to feed off it for years afterwards. It was published in a book by the RSA called *A Century of British Progress 1851–1951*, my chapter being a century of British design.

The impact of the South Bank on someone of my generation had to be experienced to be believed, for wherever one looked the hand of a designer was apparent, whether indoors or out, whether on a large scale like Ralph Tubbs's, 'Dome of

Discovery' or on a small one like Milner Gray's sign-posts; and in those days the designer's hand was indeed very different from the market—in those days a designer sought to please himself, for he was to all intents and purposes the client. And how appropriate it was that the Council of Industrial Design should have been involved in the staging of this Festival for five years before it had staged, at Sir Stafford Cripps's instigation, a miniature trial run at the Victoria and Albert Museum, at which were employed many of the designers to be re-engaged for 1951. The V & A exhibition, called 'Britain Can Make It', was in fact a preview of the 1951 South Bank with many of the same exhibits and many of the same themes. It was also very popular, attracting more than a million visitors. It proved that there was a market for designers' ideas, though it was far from proving that what the designers did was what the public wanted. But the COID pressed on with its persuasion of the public at large; it mounted exhibitions all over the country; it took space in trade shows, such as the one for the furniture industry at which it staged as a centre piece its selection of the best furniture being made; it mounted in the British Industries Fair a marvellous collection of furniture from Scotland, all of which originated from the efforts of the Scottish Committee of the COID, but most of which was ahead of its time; and it furnished houses at the Ideal Home Exhibition. On one occasion, the house being erected by the Ministry of Housing, attracted visits by the Minister, Aneurin Bevan, and Queen Mary, the former arriving punctually on site, the latter being rather late, the gap being filled by a lively discussion on design, with the Minister congratulating me on having chosen a middle-class scheme for the rooms, 'since the working classes will never get it out of their heads that the middle classes always know better how to spend their money.' All these exhibitions were staged by the head of the Council's Exhibition Division, Philip Fellows, who did more for the Council's reputation than any other member of the staff. He kept the Design Centre on its toes for some twenty-five years and took our selections of well-designed British goods to almost every capital. He was eventually awarded the OBE, an award that none could criticise.

Nye Bevan was of course a rare example—in any party—of a man who had learned to look, looking being as much a skill as doing. It had perhaps been my father who had taught him for during the war, when my widowed father was living at South End House, Montpelier Row, Twickenham, Nye, the ambitious backbencher who was determined to be Minister of Health and Housing, would spend his free Sunday afternoons talking about architecture and housing with the retired professor. I was once fortunate enough to join one of these meetings as I once was to find myself dining with my father, who had the basement flat, and Walter de la Mare, who had the attic. 'Tell me what you have been doing this week,' said my father. 'No don't tell me that, tell me what you have been thinking,' said the poet, whom I once tried to capture on tape. Professor Boris Ford, the educationist, had asked whether he could come with me one day to interview Walter de la Mare. This I fixed with some difficulty, for de la Mare was a very old and ailing man, but he was agreeable. Ford had a large clumsy tape recorder which I assumed he could work. We must have talked with de la Mare for over an hour, only to discover when we got away that the tape recorder had recorded nothing; Ford had not switched it on; but de la Mare was too old to be disturbed again.

Queen Mary was as she looked—very regal and grand, the sort of royalty to whom one did not address the first word—so, although I was supported by Aneurin Bevan, I felt fairly nervous taking her round the show house. 'What is that?' she said pointing her slender umbrella at a blackened wall in the 'teenager's room'. 'That is a blackboard, Ma'am—to encourage the child to draw.' 'It would be a bit of a bore,' she said, 'were he to begin drawing on other walls.' 'A bit of a bore' has stuck in my mind, for it seemed so far removed from the long skirt and toque hat. But I was later on to discover how human members of our Royal Family could be, the first one being

Queen Mary's daughter, Princess Mary, who rang up out of the blue to invite herself to the Design Centre that same afternoon. Gordon Russell, the director, was not available, so I went to meet the Princess and found her extremely interested and a good judge of design, particularly of table glasses; she expressed her approval of the cheapest set on display, because it would be kind to wine.

Another VIP with whom I had something to do in those early days at the COID was Harold Wilson, who came one day to Petty France when he was a very young president of the Board of Trade, to attend a meeting of the Council, strictly as an observer, for he did not speak, any more than he did when he visited an exhibition in Lewis's at Stoke-on-Trent. I found it quite interesting to discover how silent a Cabinet Minister can be on occasions off his own beat. He was much more at ease many years later when, having addressed an audience of industrialists for us as Prime Minister, he walked up Haymarket from New Zealand House where we had held our meeting, to see an exhibition in the Design Centre. The press were there with cameras which seemed to please the Prime Minister, who even made me climb into one of our model kitchens to be photographed with him. 'It is odd how prime ministers grasp at a camera as an election approaches,' said a Whitehall mandarin who witnessed it.

In the early days the COID, under Gordon Russell's direction, spent a good deal of time and effort trying to win over the retail trade. We had a splendid 'retail officer' called Jean Stewart who was succeeded by an equally effective one called Joyce Mackrell, both of whom ran courses for shopkeepers at almost all of which I had to speak; they were, though, always enjoyable for we held them in fine old houses, like Ashridge and Attingham Park, which had been converted into Adult Education Colleges. At Attingham we had the advantage of Sir George Trevelyan, the resident warden, who knew as much as we did about design and always contributed to our programmes. I am sure these retailers' courses did a lot for the cause of design, for were it possible to convert the young shopkeeper he would grow into a discriminating buyer and eventually into a caring director; and indeed we watched this happening.

We did not, however, have much success with the organisation which above all others should have set the pace—the Cooperative Movement. We certainly tried with conference after conference and store exhibition after store exhibition. We would put on courses in the Cooperative Union's school which was in a great house near Loughborough that had belonged to the chairman of a large furniture firm called Drage, but all I remember about it is that from the chairman's study one could see into the main guest bathroom through an elaborate system of mirrors. I do not believe the Co-op ever used it. I do, however, recall losing my temper when addressing a Co-op conference in Blackpool. A man at the back of the hall obviously found me boring, for he suddenly opened his newspaper and began reading. I stopped speaking and went off fuming. It was only later that I realised that the fault was probably mine, for at that time I was speaking two or three times a week and must have been boring. I doubt, though, whether with all the good will in the world we could have made much impact on the Cooperative Movement for, on one occasion, Gordon Russell and I invited the directors of the Co-op furniture factory to come and see the difference between their furniture and the furniture being made by the Swedish and Danish cooperative movements. We had all the catalogues laid out for comparison, but our guests could not see the difference. Yet it was thanks to a great Cooperator, Lord Peddie, a director of the Cooperative Wholesale Society, that ours was the first parliament in the world to discuss design, for on 17th June 1964 Lord Peddie introduced a motion in the House of Lords calling attention to the state of design in Britain and to the work of the Design Council. About eight peers joined the debate which I listened to from a gallery. They all spoke in favour of design and most of them used the notes I had prepared for their speeches.

An activity with which I was associated about this time was the Design and Industries Association's excellent exhibition of contrasting rooms at Charing Cross underground station. They were identical in shape and size, one being furnished with best sellers, the other according to the choice of Phoebe de Syllas in a forthright, though not extreme, modern manner. What made the exercise interesting was that we asked people to vote for one or the other, the ballot slip being similar to a general election one. There was also a DIA information desk manned by volunteers, one of whom was my wife. One day when she was on duty a man asked her how the voting was going. 'About ten to one in favour of the modern room;' 'Oh dear, that is not enough;' 'May I ask who you are?' 'My name is Lebus.' He was Louis Lebus, chairman of the largest furniture factory in Britain, indeed in Europe. I had once visited his Tottenham factory with him. In the design studio I saw a friend and went over to ask him what he was working on. 'Borax,' he said with disgust. Borax was a fifties expression for the worst kind of commercial furniture. When we got to the dispatch department Louis Lebus said as we looked at the shiny carcases, 'Dreadful muck, isn't it? But it is what the public wants.' He was wrong. The public did not want it and his factory closed, a fate which overtook many firms in his industry which cared little for design.

Among the original instructions to the Council in 1944 from the then President of the Board of Trade, Hugh Dalton, was the setting up of Design Centres for different industries. This idea came from the successful example of the Colour, Design and Style Centre of the Cotton Board in Manchester, but the Council was able to initiate only one Centre, that for the Rayon Industry under the directorship of the architect Dennis Lennon and his young assistant, Terence Conran. He was succeeded by Wyndham Goodden, but good as were their exhibitions the industry was not ready to support its own Design Centre; this made Gordon Russell and me begin thinking in terms of a Design Centre for British industry as a whole.

We set up a working party of senior members of the Council under the chairmanship of Sir Walter Worboys supported by Sir John Stratton then head of Dolcis, and Sir Leslie Gammage, head of the General Electricity Company. We met about three times for dinner in the Dorchester and I was asked to draft a paper on the project for submission by Walter Worboys to R. A. Butler, then Chancellor of the Exchequer. Worboys, a director of ICI, was very persuasive and Gordon Russell and I soon found ourselves looking for premises. We had the romantic idea of saving one of London's unused palaces, for what could be better than filling a fine old building with the best examples of modern design? We believed that the good of any period will sit happily with the good of any other period or rather that periods can be mixed provided they are akin in weight. Thus we looked at Spencer House quite carefully, even consulting with Lord Spencer; at Stafford House in Oxford Street; and at Forbes House at Hyde Park Corner. All three were available and central on the map of London, but Sir Edward Muir the Permanent Secretary of the Ministry of Works put his foot down for he would have been the ultimate lessor. He insisted that we should take a pavement count before deciding. The figures were insignificant, so we began looking at commercial sites, first in Bond Street and then in Haymarket. The one in Haymarket was still abuilding in 1954, having been a hole in the ground since before the war. We were promised access by 1956 for an opening date in April. We took the premises largely because buses came down not up, Haymarket, with several stopping outside the Centre. No. 28 Haymarket is as undistinguished architecturally as one could ask having been designed in the Thirties' commercial idiom without any postwar thought being applied. We had a problem, therefore, in giving ourselves an identity separate from the bulk of the building. For the outside of the Centre we chose Neville Ward who gave us a two-storeyed glass and steel face, which I was able to sell to our landlords as a distinguished addition to their building. The interior designers were the two Australian brothers, Robert and Roger Nicolson. Our brief to them was to produce an interior including exhibition fittings that would last for fifteen years. They devised a modular ceiling that lasted for more than twice that long and it was not until the late Seventies that any radical changes were made, the front being redesigned by Conran Associates and a moving staircase to the first floor shop being installed.

I once met the architect of Haymarket House at a dinner in the City and not knowing him from Adam began making some disparaging remarks about the building whereupon he confessed—a situation which I repeated at the opening of the Hilton Hotel when Conrad Hilton asked me to a party in his top floor suite from which there was a magnificent view over Hyde Park and Kensington Gardens. I asked the man whom I was standing next to who on earth could have been the architect of such a monstrous building. 'I was,' he said. My wife fell into the same trap at the opening of the Ladies' annexe to the Athenaeum Club. We bumped into an old friend, the architect Darcy Braddell, and to make conversation my wife asked him if he had seen the awful job at the Athenaeum, about which I had received an anonymous telegram: 'Ladies' Annexe now open. Presume you are resigning,' to which he replied that he had, since he had designed it.

The Design Centre began attracting foreigners right from the start, indeed from the days before the official opening, for Jane Drew and Max Fry, the distinguished architects, brought a party of Russian school teachers a day early. They were all totally fluent in English, so I asked their leader how he came to speak our language so well, to which he replied, 'Any fool can learn languages.' Even earlier visitors were Stanley Marcus and his wife from the great Neiman Marcus store in Dallas, Texas. Such an important American retailer required the director, Gordon Russell, to take him round, while I, the deputy director, looked after Mrs Marcus. I was proud to do this for the Centre was now looking very well. When we got to the white goods, I drew attention to the largest refrigerator on show. 'Yes, a dinky model,' said Mrs Marcus, thereby revealing the difference between our standards of living. The worst day for theft in the Centre's history was our first press day when we lost so many things that we had to employ a store detective who spent her time pretending to be a member of the public by wearing her hat and coat. Although she never caught a thief perhaps her presence got around for the shop-lifting fell right away and we paid her off.

'I hope that the Design Centre will now enter upon an industrious, adventurous, controversial, vitalising life, and I wish it the best of luck,' said the Duke of Edinburgh at the opening on 26 April 1956; and 'our primary objective is unashamedly commercial,' added Sir Walter Worboys, the chairman.

A few months before the official opening we organised a competition limited to the three leading graphic designers of the day—Hans Schleger, F. H. K. Henrion and Abram Games—for a symbol to help publicise the Design Centre. They each came up with solutions comprising an eye or an arrow or a square, circle and triangle. We chose Hans Schleger's solution, but it did not survive very long for we soon realised that we did not need a symbol and certainly not once we had launched our triangular black and white swing ticket for attaching to products. Over the years this ticket or label became almost the most widely recognised device in the land, second only to the wool mark. We worked very seriously on its design, seeking all manner of opinions on the right shape, colour and wording, so I have never been able to understand the decision, taken after my retirement, to sharpen the corners of the triangle.

It did not take long for the Design Centre to win its audience which rose to three, five and even on some days to ten thousand visitors. And at the same time there started the constant traffic of VIPs through the Centre—ambassadors, ministers and royalty—while I, as a senior official, had the job of waiting upon them. Some visitors were of course by our own invitation and quite formal, as when Prince Albert of Belgium came with his pretty wife to open a Belgian display on our Mezzanine floor, his speech running to ten words. 'It gives me great pleasure to declare this exhibition open,' to which Princess Margaret, who was also present, said, 'A very nice little speech,' Tony Snowdon adding, 'A little on the long side though.' Other visits were quite informal and unannounced as on that Saturday morning when I spotted Ted Heath going round making notes. I went up to him and suggested that he must be far too busy for that and would he not prefer to leave all his furnishing decisions to an expert. He agreed and I introduced him to Mrs Jo Pattrick, the wife of Michael Pattrick, the architect principal of the Central School of Art and Design. It was a good choice for she continued to work for him when he moved from Albany. Another interesting visitor was Lord Hailsham when he was Minister of Science. After touring the Centre he came to my office to meet my senior colleagues, each of whom explained what he did. Lord Hailsham's recommendation to us as he left was that we should arm ourselves with mallets 'to clock family directors over their heads'—good advice really for in many industries, particularly those involved with consumer goods, it was the family director who let the side down, going off to the South of France or elsewhere when things got difficult at home.

Mrs Thatcher came to the Centre twice during my time, once when as Secretary of State for Education she opened an exhibition from the City of Birmingham Polytechnic accompanied by her ministers Lord Eccles and Mr van Straubenzee; and earlier when, still a junior minister, she arrived in the middle of a heat wave, complained of the heat as she came in, nodded as I explained that we were continually asking the government to find us £30,000 for air conditioning, referred in her speech to the suffocating heat and nearly collapsed afterwards into my arms. We never got the £30,000 which itself was a very special *prix d'amitié* from Sir Jules Thorn. But I got my reward when many years later Mrs

17. With my daughter Victoria when she was on the *Sunday Telegraph*

18. Talking with Professor Hans Scharoun, architect of the West Berlin Concert Hall

Thatcher, the Prime Minister, gave a party-cum-seminar at No. 10 Downing Street, which she opened by referring to a lecture of mine at the Royal Court Theatre that had been her introduction to design. I recalled the occasion well for I had surveyed Chelsea, and the Cadogan Estate in particular, very thoroughly, had equipped myself with many slides of good things and bad on the estate and had then, too late, discovered that my chairman was the Earl Cadogan. He took it all very well and Mrs Thatcher apparently remembered my lecture, particularly the slides of the lamp posts.

Yet it was as Secretary of State for Education that she was most active in defence of good design. As a backbench MP she had visited Stockholm during a British Week. Her party had included my friend Lord Peddie, who told me how rightly incensed she was to see the old-fashioned image of Britain projected in the city's shop windows, and she was going back prepared to blow her top. I asked whether the three MPs—the Liberal was, I believe, Lord Amulree—had seen the COID's exhibit or the one built around our Design Index by the Swedish Cooperative Movement. They had seen neither, but were returning to London that afternoon. I persuaded them to put off their flight for one day and took them to see both shows, which certainly pacified her for they were both jolly good. Afterwards she said to me that the Council of Industrial Design would never achieve its goal until we had won the battle for design in the classrooms.

As soon as she became Secretary of State for Education, I wrote to remind her of this conversation and she invited me to call upon her in the House of Commons. There she told me that she had discovered that after all ministers have no authority over the school curricula so there was little she could do to help, but she suggested a working lunch over sandwiches in her office to which she would invite a number of headmasters and headmistresses and we would see if we could convert them. On the day this was not our problem for they were, all thirty or so of them, quite ready to agree with us that design was important;

their difficulty was the impossibility of fitting another subject into the day's work. They seemed reluctant to accept our argument that design could be introduced into history or geography lessons, as it had been at my preparatory school for, as Mrs Thatcher pointed out, the first step was to get the boys and girls to use their eyes. Not so, replied the teachers; the first step should be to get boys and girls to use their hands. We left it that I would get into touch with the Schools Council and try to persuade them to finance a design project, though Mrs Thatcher warned me that that was a long shot. I therefore called a meeting at the Design Council to which came representatives of the Schools Council, Her Majesty's Inspectors, school teachers plus a group from the Royal College of Art who were independently planning a project for teaching design in secondary schools. It was a good meeting with no contrary voices and I felt assured that, after all, the Schools Council would find the money. Eventually, however, it turned us down, so I wrote again to Mrs Thatcher who agreed to finance out of some special ministerial budget the modest proposals of the Royal College of Art.

Of course as Prime Minister she did more for design which she called 'a key factor in ensuring the economic health of the nation.' She encouraged the Department of Trade and Industry to finance what she called the Funded Consultancy Service, which provided first three million pounds, then ten and yet again ten to finance the employment of designers in industry.

The sixties were good years for the Design Council. We had held our first conference for engineers in Birmingham in 1958 under the chairmanship of Whitney Straight, at that time the Deputy Chairman of Rolls Royce, and thereafter we began paying more heed to the importance of engineering design, taking on qualified staff and mounting on the Design Centre's mezzanine floor exhibitions which drew attention to the role of the engineer designer. At the same time our work in the consumer goods industries prospered, with ever-rising attendance at the Design Centre and an ever-increasing following for what had come to be called 'contemporary' design. In 1964 the first Habitat shop opened in the Fulham Road and similar small ventures appeared in every major city, thus indicating to Terence Conran the way he should go.

It was in the sixties too that the Design Council, thanks to James Noel White, the Deputy Director, first explored the role of the artist craftsman and his relation to industrial design by putting on an exhibition called 'Hand and Machine'; indeed we made a bid to take over the ailing Crafts Centre of Great Britain thus anticipating by several years the formation of the Crafts Advisory Committee. We called a meeting in the Design Centre attended by some two hundred craftsmen but, in spite of Bernard Leach joining me on the platform and speaking in favour, they were not ready for us; they had to wait a further six years for David Eccles' initiative, which came about in a rather peculiar way. He and Sybil had asked Annette and me to dine in Barton Street. David was in bubbling good form. He eventually said that he must share his good news and told us that he had persuaded the Treasury to cough up £50,000 a year for the crafts. His problem was to find someone to spend it. The lady sitting between us at table, Lady Sandford, said surely the Council of Industrial Design was the right organisation to which David replied, 'Quite the wrong body.' We changed the subject, but a few weeks later I had a visit from the civil service head of the Office of Arts and Libraries who asked me if I was interested in the crafts. I said I was, but then told him the dinner table story to which he said that apparently the minister had changed his mind and would I please take on the job. I jumped at it for it seemed to bring nearer a long-held ambition of mine that the Design Council should cover the whole range from engineering design through industrial design to the crafts. But this was not to be. Sir Paul Sinker, the Chairman of the Crafts Advisory Committee, and I appointed Victor Margrie as secretary who, on my retirement, became director and changed the name of the organisation to the Crafts Council—but from 1971 to 1977 I was the chief executive and was thus happily involved with the staging at the Victoria and Albert Museum of the great crafts exhibition organised for us by Wyndham Goodden, an exhibition that was visited by the Duke of Edinburgh and the Prime Minister Ted Heath. I had had beforehand a little tussle with Sir John Pope Hennessey, the Director of the V & A, who was exceedingly anxious that we should put on a good show in his museum. He asked a lot of questions about Barry Mazur, our choice of designer, of whom he had never heard, so I was glad when on the opening day he asked me if Barry was free to take on other work. He was and has since done several exhibitions in the V & A.

It was in the sixties that I made contact with the Export Council for Europe which, when it eventually merged with the British National Export Council, I joined in a personal capacity. It could hardly have been a more useful contact for, apart from my joining their peripatetic team of speakers and thus being able to address all manner of industrialists in every major city in the United Kingdom, I was invited to stage a selective exhibition of good modern British design wherever they decided to hold a British Week, that is in almost every capital in Europe. And on all these occasions I met not only the staff—Sir Peter Tennant, Ion Earle, W. J. Heygate and others—but also the unpaid chairman and members of the Councils—Sir William (later Lord) McFadzean, Sir Alexander Glen, Sir Alexander Abel Smith and many others, all of whom became my friends. Once a year we would all dine together, with the Prime Minister as guest of honour, supported by many prominent industrialists and civil servants. I really doubt whether there was ever a more enthusiastic or energetic quango than the British National Export Council/ Export Council for Europe unless it were the Council of Industrial Design itself. The last ECE chairman, in succession to Sir Alexander Glen, was to become a great friend and support to me for he was Lord Caldecote who succeeded Sir Duncan Oppenheim as COID chairman in 1972. I was thus very lucky in my three chairmen, all very different from each other. The first, Sir Walter Worboys, an Australian Rhodes Scholar who became a director of ICI, was full of Aussie drive and energy and steered us through the opening of the Design Centre and me through my opening months as director; the second, Sir Duncan Oppenheim, Chairman of BAT, was as wise as he was self-effacing, a gifted painter and regular exhibitor at the Royal Academy, who disliked public speaking as much as I do but did it very well; the third Lord Caldecote, chairman of Delta Metals, took us with great aplomb and a splendid quarter-deck voice into the heart of the engineering world and supervised my changing the Council of Industrial Design into the Design Council in 1973. I was, of course, lucky in the membership of the Council most of whom were already my friends. I was able to say at my farewell dinner which also marked the twenty-first anniversary of the Design Centre and was attended by three Royal Dukes—Edinburgh, Kent and Gloucester—that 'It has indeed always surprised and delighted me that successive Secretaries of State should have had in mind for appointment to our Council exactly those names which I myself would have chosen—an example, I suppose, of Whitehall telepathy, but certainly something that has contributed remarkably to the success of our efforts.'

The only Secretary of State, in my time, to have appointed his own choice for membership was David Eccles who chose Duncan Oppenheim and Osbert Lancaster. For Duncan I became very grateful, but Osbert was an exceptionally bad attender, though he endeared himself to me at his first meeting by asking me whether I was the son of 'that great and good man, Charles Reilly'.

6

First Visit to Russia

Sir Gordon Russell used to complain in his uncomplaining way about the amount of foreign travel I managed to fit into a year. I suppose he had some grounds for this because I visited every country in Europe and indeed every continent, usually with my wife, for foreign travel alone is not enjoyable. One of our first jaunts was to Paris to attend a conference organised by Jacques Vienot at which I spoke in French about the Council of Industrial Design and which thereafter was always claimed inaccurately by the French as the first ever international gathering on design, the first one having actually been in London two years earlier as a feature of the Festival of Britain. My early expeditions, however, were normally on my own, such as my trips to Germany for the British Council, where I spoke in English to audiences in Die Brücke, in Berlin, Hanover and Cologne, or my first post war trip to Sweden and Finland where I lectured to audiences assembled by the Svenskaslödjforeningen and by Ornamo and where I came under the spell of Scandinavian designers.

It was in 1952 in Helsinki, for instance, that I met the then Public Relations Officer of Arabia, Olof Gummerus, who later became the man in charge of promoting Finnish design around the world; he was more English than an Englishman, speaking our language faultlessly, sporting a red buttonhole and in England a bowler hat. He it was who took me to see the top floor craftsmen at Arabia, explaining that each one had an entirely free hand to produce what he or she wanted in the hope that they would inspire the workers down below. Among these craftsfolk was the little bird-like Rut Bryk, the wife of the famous Tapio Wirkkala, the master designer in wood, glass, ceramics, steel—indeed in any material for any purpose—who grew more bear-like with every year and became a national, even international institution. These two designers were very typical of Finland for not only did they work in many widely different fields, Rut being as good a weaver as she is a ceramist, but both were craftsmen first and industrial designers second, both belonged to the generation that sought to revitalise machine production through the injection of hand-made quality. They and their many colleagues like Timo Sarpaneva, Ilmari Tapiovaara, Dora Jung, Kaj Franck and Antti Nurmesniemi and his wife Vuokko, were the people who won for Finland the world-wide reputation for imagination and skill in all the applied arts. It was my great good fortune to get to know them and to become their friend, just as it was my good luck to meet and make friends with the creative folk in Sweden, Denmark and Norway; indeed our frequent visits to Scandinavia have greatly enriched our lives, one of the most rewarding having been in 1957 when we went first to Denmark where we were warmly entertained by Erik Herlow, Acton Björn, Sören Hanson and others before being shipped to Norway where we met Arne and Grete Korsmo, the leading modern architect and marvellous silversmith, and where we struck the Kräfta season and guzzled our way through dish after dish of crayfish, repeating the performance in Sweden and then Finland.

It was in Helsinki that Annette and I received our first invitation to visit Russia. It came from my cousins, Sir Patrick and Lady Reilly, at that time occupying the British Embassy where Patrick was our ambassador. We jumped at it and took a Finnair plane to Moscow Vouknovo airport where Patrick and Rachel met us and we had our first sight of a Russian interior. To my eyes it looked about fifty years out of date, at least for an airport, with its heavy drapes at the windows, its sort of carpet on the table, its cut glass on the carpet and its old-fashioned, upholstered furniture in which we sat while our luggage was cleared. We had been asked in the plane to fill in a long questionnaire of which one question was how much hashish we were importing.

The first impression of driving into Moscow was the immense width of the road, a feature we were to discover in all sectors of the city; some had been widened in Stalin's time by the removal of houses between two, thereby more than doubling the remaining road and thus affording a clear field of fire, as it is very difficult to organise any kind of uprising in straight wide streets. It was on that first drive in that I saw my first examples of socialist-realist architecture, great multi-corniced blocks loaded with pseudo-renaissance detail or else neo-classical paraphernalia of the coarsest kind. We were staying in the Embassy opposite the Kremlin, but we saw the vacant lot intended for our new building and we thanked our stars that bureaucracies move slowly.

Patrick told me that he was assuming that I wished for a busman's holiday, that he had been unable to find in any reference book any mention of a body that might correspond with the Council of Industrial Design, but that he had arranged a meeting for me in two days' time with the Chairman of the State Committee for Science and Technology, a man called Maxaryev, who was a minister and a candidate member of the Praesidium. The office of this State Committee was No. 11 Gorky Street. When I drove there I was greeted on the pavement by a young man speaking perfect English who told me that his chairman was a very busy man but would see me for five minutes; so up we went in their old lift where another man attached himself to us as did a third and fourth before we reached the chairman's office, a vast room with a dais at the far end on which stood a great desk surmounted by an enormous inkwell—inkwells being in the Soviet Union what carpets are in Whitehall. Maxaryev himself was far taller than most Russians, so when he stood up to make his opening remarks he looked down on the rest of us who were all seated at a long table at right angles to his desk in very low chairs; my eyes were just about level with the top of his desk. After an exchange of words of welcome, I plunged right in and asked him if the words 'industrial design' meant anything to him. He shook his head as did his supporters, so I asked why they were building their new world with the cast off symbols of our old one. He did not much like that and asked me to explain myself, so I said that from what I had been able to see in two days in Moscow their new buildings were what we in the West would call 'reactionary, bourgeois, capitalist, banker's taste'—I paused duly on each word to ensure their translation. I feared he might close the interview, but instead he stood up, came round his desk, moved his staff down one place, ordered soft drinks and cigarettes and sat himself opposite me. 'Now,' he said, 'tell me about your organisation.' 'But you have only five minutes.' 'We have time,' and indeed he did, for that first conversation lasted ninety minutes and at the end he asked me to come back the day after tomorrow to see an exhibition of the things I had been criticising and to meet the designers who had been responsible and would I please speak as frankly to them as I had to him, the minister who had never drawn a line. I promised and returned to the Embassy quite pleased with my first meeting.

Two days later I returned to Gorky Street and was taken to an immense room which had been turned into an exhibition gallery with photographs on pin-up panels all round the outside and in the middle a group of some twenty men with the Minister, who explained that I would like to talk to each of them about their work. It was rather like an architectural school 'crit' with the visiting examiner doing his round. When I got to the locomotive engineer I saw a photograph of a very familiar thing, an engine with speed whiskers and stream-lining like Raymond Loewy's for the Pennsylvania Railway. When I asked why he had done that, was it because the Americans had, I felt a tug on my arm and an interpreter said, 'Mr Soloviev would like to speak with you.' Soloviev was the senior designer present. He said to me, 'We are not proud of what we are showing you. We can do better than this,' so I hurried round the rest of the room and then asked the Minister whether I might spend some time with Soloviev, a man who thought as I did. Maxaryev agreed, said that he would put a car at our disposal, told me that I could see anything I wanted, but made a condition—that we should be accompanied by Mr Germen Gvishiani who spoke English, Soloviev having none. Gvishiani was a young Georgian looking like a youthful Stalin with a black moustache and thick black hair. It was only when I came to read Robert Conquest's *The Great Terror* that I learned that his father had been M. M. Gvishiani, the head of the NKVD in the Maritime Province.

Next day the three of us climbed into a black Zim limousine and set off. Gvishiani asked me, to my surprise, whether I was a follower of Sir Herbert Read or of Lewis Mumford, a nice question which I could answer without difficulty since only three weeks earlier we had entertained both of them at our house in South Kensington, Herbert Read having spoken for freedom and self expression, Lewis Mumford for a healthy, positive, affirmative approach to art, but it was a surprising opening to several days discussion in Moscow. We packed in as much as possible—visits to exhibitions, factories and committees—and all the time talking among ourselves, building confidence and friendship. I still get New Year cards from Gvishiani now a Moscow mandarin, an academician, vice-chairman of his State Committee, son-in-law of the late Prime Minister Kosygin, while Yuri Soloviev has over the years become one of my closest though distant friends.

I would return each evening to the Embassy telling Patrick all about my adventures. He said I had probably talked with more Russians in my six days than he had in his first six weeks. At the end he agreed to support my suggestion that my two Russian companions should be invited to London. This idea occurred to me when we were looking at an exhibition of building materials which included some show houses and flats. These were so run down and ill kempt that Gvishiani started criticising before I did. He begged me to write a piece for one of their papers. I said it would be better still for them to pay a visit to London to see our '*Daily Mail* Ideal Home Exhibition', then in its hey day, and they jumped at the idea. So it came about that they were invited by the Foreign Office and British Council and both accepted.

Life in the Embassy in those days was not easy for, apart from the perpetual anxiety about bugging which meant our walking up and down the lawn well away from the trees for any confidential conversation, the domestic staff in the Embassy were all Russians, except for the cook. Our visit coincided with one by Nye Bevan and Jenny Lee, for whom my cousins organised a dinner with a fresh salmon flown in from Helsinki. It was then that we realised the appalling difficulties under which ambassadresses lived behind the Iron Curtain, for it was not till after five o'clock that news came through that Mr A. I. Mikoyan would be the chief Russian guest and it was not until he arrived that it was known how many he would bring with him, one of whom was his interpreter, who spoke such idiomatic English that I mistook him for an Englishman. I see him still, though greyer, acting as an interpreter at various televised summits and meetings with British VIPs. The most memorable features of that first dinner in the British Embassy were Mr Mikoyan's greeting, hands together Indian fashion, and Jenny Lee's firm refusal to leave the table before the men.

My first visit to a Russian factory was to a large one making nasty shiny furniture just like the bottom end of our own industry. Near the entrance was a group of large photographs of workers who had done well, but to my eyes the pictures were all rather old as if the competition had lost its way and to be chosen as a Stakhanovite no longer had much appeal. The factory itself was no more and no less interesting than similar ones at home, but the management's hospitality was dangerously lavish—vodka after vodka interspersed with Armenian brandy until I could hardly stand. I think they enjoyed a visiting fireman for he was a good excuse for some heavy drinking. When I protested that I had to get back to our Embassy for lunch they produced their *pièce de résistance*—slices of orange heaped with icing sugar. They assured me that to eat such a mixture would entirely obliterate any smell of alcohol. It failed completely according to my wife for the vodka or the smell of it was coming out of my skin.

A much soberer visit was to the committee which decided which textiles were to go into production. The chairman was a blue serge-suited woman nearly as broad as she was tall; she was supported by three or four of each sex who were all in suits and sat very formally round a table. We asked to see samples of what they were proposing for the coming season and then to compare them with the current production. There was almost no difference, thus reinforcing to my mind the extraordinary conservatism of the Soviet Union.

Two sightseeing trips in the Embassy car took us to Zagorsk, a city of churches of which some were in use and in one of which we saw a corpse in an open coffin being paraded around; and Svenigorod, a smaller church inside castle walls capping a small hill. Patrick pointed out that when on top of the hill there would be nothing higher to the west until Aldeburgh.

Our return journey was fairly hair-raising. Patrick had cleverly booked us most economically on an Aeroflot plane to Berlin, which flew in and out of cloud the whole way, the first stop being at Vilnius, where we had a ghastly breakfast of last night's reheated veal and veg in a typical Stalinist temple of an airport. Then on to Warsaw where we got mixed up with the military reception for the visiting President of Outer Mongolia. We had had about half an hour in Warsaw airport when we saw our plane taxiing off towards the runway. The plane was gathering speed when the last passenger clambered in. Our arrival at East Berlin was carefully filmed as we walked down from the aeroplane. This was, of course, before the Wall had been built so there was no problem in finding a taxi to take us into West Berlin where our English speaking driver (he had been a prisoner of war) sought an hotel. Our stay in West Berlin enabled us not only to have a good look at Interbau, the permanent exhibition of modern architecture with all the great international names contributing a building, but also to attend a congress organised by the German equivalent of the COID at which I was to speak in the great new Congress Hall built at American expense but since, I believe, pulled down. This time I spoke in German.

That was the first of our visits to Berlin to be followed by several more, one of which took us through the Wall. I had been invited to speak at the opening of the International Design Centre in West Berlin and was staying with Annette in the Hotel am Zoo at which a telegram arrived reading:

> ERWARTEN SIE UND IHRE GATTIN AM
> SONNABEND UM 10 UHR AM
> AUSLAENDERUEBERGANG FRIEDRICHSTRASSE
> CHECK POINT CHARLIE—signed FRIEDLAENDER

Not knowing this Friedlaender from Adam we took courage and mackintoshes (for it was pouring with rain) and presented ourselves at the monstrous Wall. In due course we found ourselves, like two spies going back into the cold, in a sort of uninhabited no man's land behind the minefields, tank trips and barbed wire. For a moment or two we wondered what on earth we were doing there, when, to our relief, two figures detached themselves from a building opposite and walked towards us. We met in the middle of the drenched, empty crossroads and were taken on a tour of the vast new workers' dwellings of East Berlin, ending up in a comfortable bourgeois restaurant where several German designers were awaiting us including Dr Martin Kelm, Director of the East German COID. We returned by the still running electric train which passed through several pre-war railway stations still carrying their pre-war enamelled tin advertisements.

Shorty before my Russian friends were due to arrive at Heathrow I heard that Gvishiani was not coming so I had to find an interpreter through the FO and with him I went to fetch Yuri Soloviev. It was a Saturday in March 1958. We went straight to the Design Centre which to my great delight was so crowded we could not get in—a good demonstration of the popularity of modern design and one I enjoyed showing to a Communist visitor. We went to have tea at the almost empty Athenaeum club so that he could see another side of life in Britain. I had organised a very full programme for Soloviev, visiting schools, exhibitions, factories and travelling to Stoke-on-Trent and High Wycombe; Mr Lucien Ercolani (the founder) showed him with great pride round the Ercol factory at High Wycombe, but not before he had been introduced to all the shop stewards, who confirmed unanimously that they could afford to buy the furniture that they were making and indeed did so. This impressed Soloviev for Ercol furniture was infinitely better than its Russian equivalent. I did not go to Stoke-on-Trent, but the interpreter told me how Soloviev had insisted on stopping to take some photographs of a roadside gypsy encampment no doubt proving thereby something about British standards of living, though Gvishiani had carefully explained to me in Moscow that British standards were two and a half times higher than the Russian, and American two and a half times higher than the British.

I did not really expect to see Soloviev again, but I wrote to him sending him the 1958 COID annual report and jokingly telling him that they should set up a Design Council in Russia. I got no answer, but in 1961 I had a letter from him telling me that they had taken my advice, had established with Khrushchev's blessing an Institute for Industrial Design and that he had been appointed director of the Institute. About this time I met the Russian ambassador Soldatov and asked him whether he had met Soloviev. He had not, but said to me, 'I know you have for you invented him.' A little while later I received another letter, this time from Gvishiani, inviting me and my wife to Russia in exchange for my giving some lectures, the details to be worked out between Soloviev and myself. So in September 1962 we returned to Russia where we were met by Soloviev, now speaking good English. We had some trouble at the airport for my visa had been wrongly dated by the Russian Embassy in London and had apparently expired on the very day of our arrival, but Soloviev, revealing surprising authority, soon sorted that out and took us to our hotel in Leningradski Prospect, the Sovietskaya. It was a very large building with plenty of Stalinist architecture. We were given a suite of five rooms, but even so the hotel struck me as a really old fashioned dump, excellent as was the vodka and caviar, so I was quite surprised when next day at the British Embassy our Ambassador, Sir Frank Roberts, having asked where we were living said, on hearing the Sovietskaya, 'Good Lord, they are doing you well; that's where they normally put up people like Aneurin Bevan.' So I asked Soloviev why we were being so well treated and he replied, 'Because mine is a grade one institute.' It seemed that Russian hospitality was graded according to the host, not the guest. Soloviev further explained that he had surprised his father, the designer of the aero-engines used in Ilyushin planes, who betted that the Institute for Industrial Design would be graded fourth class, while Yuri Soloviev was sure that it would come out on top. Of course when we went to the Institute we were not so impressed; it was in an over-decorated building on the edge of the Park of Economic Achievement, but there was a model of the new building—a glass box—that was planned for the future.

We called on Gvishiani on our first morning. He was obviously on his way up, but I was glad for Soloviev that he and his Institute had been put under that State Committee for clearly Gvishiani liked him and science and technology were the coming subjects. Fortunately I had brought some slides illustrating the COID's interest in technology and was able to show them next evening in Kiev. I could see from the reaction of the man in charge of pottery and glass in the Kiev region that Soloviev was going to have just as hard a time as I had in persuading industry to his point of view, for the industrialist laughed quite openly at the idea of someone coming from Moscow to tell him what to do; he felt quite capable of deciding what to make. Soloviev, however, urged me in my lecture to bear in mind that I would be talking in the context of a consumers' strike, and to prove his point took us to a pottery and glass shop where the shelves were stocked with such awful designs that no one visited the place. It was in Kiev that we saw our first Russian glass works, a large affair staffed by both sexes with mixed chairs and instead of human lungs rubber bladders for blowing—but, alas, it was a case of death by a thousand cuts (as Lord Conesford used to say) for every piece had to be decorated. They showed us with pride their small sick bay staffed by a couple of women in white, but otherwise as old fashioned and unhygienic as possible, indeed very like a great chemist's shop that I had to visit which was fitted with pre-revolutionary shelves and cupboards, all of them empty, but standing proudly round the top large glass bottles filled with coloured liquids. I had caught pink eye and needed some drops which were administered by a woman in a white overall, but the bottle was then wrapped in newspaper before being handed to me—a strange mixture of today and yesterday, which we were to come across frequently on our tour. Soloviev used to say that Russia was the only country in the world in which one could live in six centuries at once.

The next day we had to go to Kiev airport where we were kept waiting for several hours for a plane which did not turn up, but Soloviev ordered us a splendid meal of caviar, vodka and grilled sturgeon in a private room; the lavatories, however, were so disgustingly dirty that we had to go in the woods at the edge of the airport. These filthy toilets were in those days everywhere in Russia, in the air as on the ground, while wherever one found oneself in a crowd of people there was always the overpowering smell of armpits and old socks. When the aeroplane turned up it took us only as far as Rostov, where we had to change planes, the one we climbed into having well worn tyres and a fuselage full of peasants, four of whom were turned out to make way for our party. It came down in a hurry in the Caucasus at a small airport called Mineralyevode and burst

19. HRH The Duke of Edinburgh taking the chair of his elegance panel with Sir Robin Darwin, Lady Casson, Mrs Gaby Schreiber and Sir Basil Spence

20. Judging a furniture competition with Enrico Peressuti, John Reid, Arne Jacobsen and Charles Eames

21. Receiving the Compasso d'Oro from Sir Ashley Clarke and Count Aldo Borletti in Milan in 1960

22. With my cousin Sir Patrick Reilly, GCMG

its tyres on touchdown. Thus we spent most of the night squatting on our luggage while they fitted new tyres, and it was not until about 4 a.m. that we reached our destination, Baku, where to our astonishment our reception committee was still waiting for us, armed with flowers and fruit.

The next day I had a meeting with a local party boss, who turned out to be a woman. She told us that they were proud in Azerbaijan of their craftsmanship and it would be well received if, in my lecture that evening, I could make some reference to the importance of craftsmanship. I recalled a nice quotation from Confucius which I had originally discovered on the back of a lavatory door in a Sheffield factory. It seems that Confucius was asked how he would recognise a good craftsman. He replied, 'First by the reputation of his ancestors for honesty and sincerity; secondly by his ability to create something new with his traditions that are old.' So I thought I would try this out on my interpreter. 'But Confucius was Chinese, wasn't he?' she said; 'Yes, but does that matter?' I replied; 'Must you use a Chinese quotation?' she said, thus revealing the extent of the gulf between the two countries, a gulf that had been shown up by Soloviev in Moscow when we were dining in the National Hotel at a table next to a party of Chinese. 'Friends of yours?' I said, to which he replied, 'That was a very bad joke.'

Our days in Baku were filled with new experiences—a bathe in the Caspian Sea, as warm as a morning bath but smelling strongly of oil; a drive through an oil field with, in all directions, nodding pumps working away unattended; an evening ballet built round a very simple story of princes and peasants, the former wicked, the latter good; an open air performance by a troupe from Poland, who were returning next day to Moscow with Soloviev in attendance, we three—Annette, myself and our interpreter, Ludmilla—going on to Sochi to get a view of Russians packed like sardines on the beach, all slowly turning pink and most of them very fat.

Our last stop of the tour was Leningrad at the end of a long flight from the Black Sea to the Baltic, with Ludmilla doing her best to make us feel at ease. Our hotel, the Europa, was certainly rather grand—a pre-revolutionary place, with plenty of panelling and wrought iron and once more we were given a suite of rooms. My lecture in Leningrad was to the local school of art. It was a large audience of both sexes and at the end of my talk the chairman who was the headmaster told me he would ask for questions but there would be none; he would then leave the platform but would I please stay. 'You will get plenty of questions,' he said. So I did as I was told and how right he was. I was surrounded by eager young people wanting to know if students in England were really at liberty to do what they wanted, if a student could get something of his own put into production and if so could he keep the proceeds? They were much more interested in economics than in design and I was quite ready to make their mouths water.

We managed a good deal of conventional Leningrad sight-seeing, the most surprising piece being the enormous Scythian Treasure in the Hermitage. We had never seen so much gold before or such minuscule workmanship which required a magnifying glass to see the marvellous detail. Our journey back to Moscow was by the famous Red Arrow train, another piece of outdated equipment like the Tupolev planes which had carried us round Russia. Annette and I had first class tickets and were therefore together in our sleeping compartment. Ludmilla went off to find her berth, but was back in no time and very agitated. She had found a great naked hairy man fast asleep in her bottom bunk. She begged my wife to come along and see for herself, which she did. My wife said she was sure I would swop bunks but at that moment we saw the large uniformed figure of the female attendant and suggested that Ludmilla should ask whether it was right to put a young married woman in the same compartment as a naked man. Eventually she was found a berth at a safe distance from the hairy Russian and we all had a good night, but the incident bore out a story we had heard of the risks of Russian railway travel.

7

Journeys in the Sixties and Seventies

Thus began a long connection with Eastern Europe thanks to the Foreign Office which financed exhibitions of modern British design in all the capitals. I am sure that none of this would have happened had it not been for the lead given by the Soviet Union, for no sooner had Russia established its own design organisation than similar bodies grew up in all her satellites, mostly closely modelled on the Russian prototype. The Poles, however, were the first to invite an exhibition from London's Council of Industrial Design. This was in 1963 and served as a model for all future shows. Our official host was a charming lady called Zofia Szydlowska who spoke good French. She seemed to hold a ministerial rank, which she had achieved through having been in the same prison as Poland's then boss, Mr Gomulka; they managed to get to know each other through tapping messages on iron pipes and Gomulka rewarded her with office when he came to power, even though she was a former aristocrat. Our exhibition was planned by the COID's exhibition officer, Philip Fellows, erected by the Central Office of Information and supervised on site by Fellows's assistant, John Branch, who had a strange experience in his hotel bedroom; he suddenly noticed his telephone moving of its own accord, the hand set lifting up and listening. My wife and I also had our first experience of Iron Curtain surveillance. We found that someone had ripped out the linings of our suitcases.

1964 was the year of our first exhibition in Moscow. Soloviev had explained to me that he did not want a 'way of life' show, but one that would emphasize the technological aspects of design. I, of course, wanted to make Russian mouths water. We appointed Terence Conran to design the exhibition, which he did very well, spending long hours with his sleeves rolled up, actually putting the exhibits into position. In the result both sides were well pleased, Soloviev congratulating us on sticking to his rules, I being very well satisfied at the public reaction to those parts of the exhibition which demonstrated our standard of living. I had arranged with our people to keep a count of the visitors and was not surprised to hear that we had passed half a million, for the Russians came in eight abreast from morning till night. I was, though, quite surprised to be called back to Moscow at the end of the exhibition to greet the two hundred thousandth visitor. Being called back, however, did give me the opportunity to put right a mistake I had made. My wife and I were staying at the British Embassy as guests of Sir Humphrey and Lady Trevelyan and Humphrey asked me what present I had brought for Mr Victor Rudnev, the Chairman of the State Committee for Science and Technology and thus Soloviev's boss. I said I had a fine canteen of stainless steel cutlery. 'Stainless steel,' said Humphrey, 'that's no good. It must be silver.' So on my return to Moscow I had with me a beautiful silver cigarette box made by Gerald Benney, which I duly took round to No. 11 Gorky Street to present when I went to see the chairman, who asked me, after glancing without much interest at Gerald Benney's undecorated simple box, whether the COID had difficulty in persuading manufacturers to exhibit in the Design Centre. 'No,' I said, 'they seem very keen to get in. All they have to do is to improve their product.' 'Unfortunately,' he replied, 'that would not be possible under our system.' So I asked him why not and he explained that Soviet industrialists, being very conservative, would find it hard to change their patterns; so I referred him to Harold Wilson, who at that moment was fighting an election in Britain and was threatening to nationalise any companies that were unwilling to change things for the better. I suggested that the Soviet Union should take a leaf out of Wilson's book, but in the opposite sense; they should encourage private enterprise to compete with sluggish state concerns. 'And that,' said Rudnev laughing, 'would certainly not be possible under our system.' As we left the room, I said to Gvishiani, 'That was surely rather dangerous talk to have in Moscow?' to which he replied, 'Safety starts at the top.'

Two further points about that exhibition are perhaps worth recalling, one at the start, the other at the end. The first, the opening by Sir Humphrey Trevelyan speaking fluent Russian, was attended by several Members of Council of the Council of Industrial Design who had flown out specially, such as Sir Roger Falk, Sir Misha Black, Anthony Heal and Mrs Elspeth Juda; most were visiting Russia for the first time; they all attended a splendid Anglo-Russian supper at our Embassy at which Humphrey made an excellent speech in Russian which was obviously full of jokes to judge from the laughter of the Russian guests. The second event on the final day of the show was the rape of the British Exhibition, for the crowds must somehow have sensed the end and so descended in their thousands, removing everything that was pocketable or detachable, every knob, every handle, every screw.

However before that day my wife and I had fitted in a visit to Czechoslovakia as guests of an organisation with the initials UBOK. We were met at the airport in Prague by an architect called Gocar, whose father had been host before the war to a party from the Architectural Association which I had joined because Derek Bridgwater, my brother-in-law, was a member. We had visited not only old Prague but all the new buildings, particularly the ones by Havlincek and Honzig, the two most successful modern architects of those days, who later recanted under the Germans and produced some very bad stuff. We had also been to Zlin, the great Bata headquarters, and to Brnö, where we had been entertained by Doctor Tugendhat in his splendid villa designed by Mies van der Rohe, to both of which we were taken again in 1964, Zlin having been renamed Gottwaldov, after the first communist boss of Czechoslovakia, and the villa Tugendhat having been turned into a nursery school. A great advantage of being first cousin to Sir Patrick Reilly was the entrée the kinship gave me to British embassies, so we soon found ourselves hobnobbing with Sir Cecil and Lady Parrott in the magnificent embassy in Prague in which I was later to stay on several occasions with Lord Snowdon. One of the first questions that Cecil Parrott asked me was where we were staying. When I named our hotel—I think it was the Flora—he said, 'Goodness, I would not put my servants there,' which was a fair comment indicating the humble status of UBOK, our Czech hosts. But however humble, they did their best for us, driving us round their beautiful countryside, taking us to Bratislava from whose castle we could clearly see the Slovak–Austrian frontier with its barbed wire and watch-towers and to Karlovy Vara where we were given a rose coated with salt from the spa waters as a souvenir of our visit. But the real souvenir was the pathetic state of the villages through which we drove, a state that was to be rendered by contrast even more deplorable a year or so later when I visited Philip Rosenthal at Selb just over the frontier in West Germany, where everything was spick and span.

We were later to find the same down-at-heel squalor in every farming community in Bulgaria, the reason in both countries being the absence of private ownership. We had seen the same blight in Poland when we drove from Warsaw to Cracow and would no doubt have seen it in Russia had we not travelled everywhere by air. It was in Czechoslovakia that we first realised the cost of Communism, for it was in Prague that we saw row upon row of empty pre-1948 shops, with here and there a fly-blown, unloved window containing a few tins or other odd assortments of socialist productivity. It made one realise the richness of the ordinary English high street, while a visit to one of their larger stores made one really appreciate a western supermarket. It was therefore not surprising that we could in the next year or so stage in Prague an exhibition to render British design the cynosure of Czech eyes and to stir

UBOK to increased activity; indeed in a few years we were able to invite a Czech exhibition to London's Design Centre, having first been out to Prague again, this time with Lord Snowdon, to ensure a reasonable selection.

Lord Snowdon's English sports car, a convertible Aston Martin, driven to Czechoslovakia by his chauffeur, attracted a great deal of attention, although Tony found it rather strange, I believe, not to be recognised by anyone. The car, though, was a symbol of excellence which underlined the difference between East and West, and brought home to me the extraordinary collapse of standards in Czechoslovakia since the war. On my pre-war visit, Prague had been a model city with the smartest of shops and hotels and breathtakingly beautiful women. Under Communism all was drab and neglected with women almost universally clothed in plastic mackintoshes. We were to see the same low-grade shop windows and same uglification wherever we went in Hungary or Bulgaria or Roumania. Indeed getting to Bucharest was itself like putting the clock back, for our British Airways plane had to come down at Sofia on account of the famous Balkan fog and we were offered the choice of waiting until it cleared or taking a night train. I chose the train and spent twelve hours travelling some two hundred miles, the reason being that the old steam engine needed refuelling at frequent intervals, not with coal but with wood which was laid alongside the tracks in neatly stacked piles. The train itself seemed to have travelled across Europe, starting somewhere in Poland—at least there was a friendly Pole in one of the four bunks in my compartment, the other two being occupied by a properly hirsute Roumanian and a bearded Nigerian who slipped next door to keep a pretty young black girl company.

It was in Bucharest that I met the young Romanian designers who had won a prize for designing a poster to advertise our exhibition and who a year later with only one passport between them bravely escaped on a motorcycle via Bulgaria and Yugoslavia to Austria, the Bulgarians letting them through to annoy the Roumanian authorities for whom they have no love. The two designers—Olimpia and Eugen Nicolcev—stayed with us in London on their way to Canada, where they soon fell on their feet, but not without explaining to us what I had already suspected in Bucharest, that the Roumanian system is the cruellest, most Stalinist of all in Eastern Europe, which allows their government the possibility of appearing to stand up to the Russians, thereby misleading the West into believing Roumania to be a weak link in the Soviet chain.

For all the ugliness of Eastern Europe, all the smell that hits one on entering the airport, all the backwardness in design, we found wherever we went friendship and smiling faces and even in Russia an eagerness to swop experiences and to indulge in frank exchanges. I remember once flying from Tblisi to Moscow and then on from Moscow to Belgrade. We changed planes at Moscow, leaving Aeroflot and boarding the Yugoslav airline JAT. I noticed on boarding how smiling and cheerful the Yugoslavian stewardesses were and said to my Russian neighbour how different these girls were from those on board the Aeroflot plane and what was the reason? He replied immediately, 'Our girls are afraid,' to which I replied, 'Surely not—your planes are all quite safe aren't they?' To which he replied, 'They are afraid of the system,' and then almost at once, 'We *all* are.'

The jolliest, friendliest people we came across in Russia were the Georgians and Armenians, both great drinkers of their own brews, in Georgia wines, in Armenia brandies, and both strict adherents to the tradition of toasting, particularly in the presence of foreigners. Half-way through my first big dinner in Tblisi it was my turn to give a toast, the twenty-sixth of the evening so, hoping to draw the assembly to a close, I proposed the health of the chef. This seemed to spur him to further effort for he produced another twenty dishes, each the excuse for another toast. The toastmaster or Tamada for the evening was a Bulgarian whom we got to know well later on when we were invited to Bulgaria. He was called Minko Hassimsky, whose first name we borrowed for a little Pekinese dog, an earlier Peke having also carried the name of a designer friend, Tapio, from Tapio Wirkkala.

Our main reason for visiting Tblisi, which we did three times at two or three year intervals, was of course to see what was going on at the Georgian branch of the All Union Institute for Industrial Design or VNIITE to use its Russian acronym; and to our surprise what was going on remained the same over the six or seven years. On our first visit the couple of hundred staff were working on a design for a 'new' petrol station for use on the new highways that were to be built to cope with the new cars being produced by the new Fiat factory. There was, though, going to be nothing new about their petrol station for they were studying piles of catalogues and leaflets of pumps produced in the West. On our second visit no progress had been made but some new catalogues had appeared and were being read and copied. Next time, unbelievably, it was the same story, the reason being, I was told, because the staff were considered too incompetent to design anything themselves. It was a repetition of the Moscow story. The VNIITE headquarters were for ever designing a new taxi which never got beyond the prototype stage and certainly not into production.

On one of my trips to Tblisi I was accompanied by three distinguished Americans. On the way from Moscow I flew with Henry Dreyfuss, the famous industrial designer, who had a tiny camera which took pictures sideways so that when pointing his camera across the table at me he was in fact recording what was visible out of the window, a dangerous pastime in Russia. We were flying in an old Tupolev which had all the accoutrements that one used to find in the pre-war Brighton Belles. After studying it all for a while, Henry said how nervous he felt surrounded by so much handwork; much safer to fly in a proper piece of industrial production. On the way back to Moscow I sat with Buckminster Fuller but, alas, he was suffering from flu so we did not have the conversation that we should have had. When in Tblisi we organised an evening gathering of Anglo-American and Russian designers—a sort of free for all with the Russians emphasizing their belief in productivity and the Americans begging them to desist. The leading American in this discussion was the very articulate Edgar Kaufman Jr who argued forcibly against the importance of possessions, while the Russians argued as forcibly in favour. As I listened I felt that the Russians were suffering from object starvation, the Americans from object saturation, while the English perhaps were enjoying object satisfaction.

Georgia and Armenia were linked for us by the existence of the most remarkable ancient churches. We lit candles in one of the oldest in Georgia and in Armenia we watched animals being sacrificed at the high altar, but only edible ones, for after ritual blood letting they were taken out to a cloister where they were cooked and eaten. A further link for us between the two republics was that we crossed the frontier on foot, walking the last mile or so along a deserted highway towards our Armenian car, which drove us to an open air restaurant, where we were charged with brandy instead of wine and where Annette made her first speech in the Soviet Union. Our hotel in Yerevan, though the grandest in the city, was infested by bugs about which we lodged a complaint the next morning with the local Communist Party headquarters. The Armenians themselves, however, could not have been friendlier or more outspoken in their condemnation of the Soviet system under which they had to spend their days having been misled by Khrushchev's propaganda and thus enticed away from their homes in Egypt and Palestine where those whom we met had all learned to speak English and even to sing in it. Our last evening we were escorted round the main square of Yerevan with our Armenian hosts singing 'Rule Britannia'. Next morning we were seen off at the airport by the same cheerful group, but with children present, one boy wearing a blue blazer with our British royal coat of arms emblazoned on his breast pocket. This time they sang 'God Save the Queen'.

The sixties and seventies were good years for the Design Council or rather for its director for he was invited everywhere to speak about the Council's work, to open exhibitions and to open design centres modelled on the London prototype. In these years Britain's reputation stood very high, not perhaps for design, but at least for effort. I suppose our longest foreign trip was to Japan, Hong Kong, New Zealand and Australia, the flight to Japan passing over Russia and stopping for a short while in Moscow's new international airport. Our Japanese hosts were the Industrial Products Research Institute who certainly made me sing for my supper, each lecture lasting up to three hours because the Japanese translations took so long, but each audience being very well disciplined and attentive. The most memorable feature of that first visit was an expedition to Matchiko to call upon the great living treasure of Japan, the potter Shoji Hamada, whom I had met with Bernard Leach in London. He lived on an estate comprising several patrician houses which he had brought from different parts of Japan, a feat made possible since each house was built of wood. He was kind enough to give me one of his pots and to allow our guide to photograph him doing so. One of the houses, which he showed us with great pride, was used as a storehouse for his collection of English furniture, not by any means a collection that would entrance an Englishman, for it comprised the most ordinary commercial pieces. It made me wonder how often Westerners are misled when buying *objets d'art* in the Orient.

Before we left Japan we met a designer called Bin Kuwahara who later turned up in London and telephoned my wife saying that she had nowhere to stay, so we asked her to come to us for a short while, which eventually became eight months. We were well rewarded, not only by her friendship but by her and her husband's extraordinary generosity to us when we next went to Japan for an ICSID Congress. They looked after us for a few days after the Congress, taking us to Nara and Yoshino, where we spent the night in the Japanese Inn that was a favourite of the Emperor before the war, and to Hakone where we greatly enjoyed the open air sculpture park with its outstanding Henry Moore and its two good pieces by Hiromori Kuwahara, Bin's husband. The Yoshino Inn, cantilevered over a sheer drop of several hundred feet, was as good an example as one could ask of a typical, traditional Japanese building: *tatamis* everywhere, silently sliding partitions and a bath the size of a small bedroom, into which we plunged after carefully washing ourselves all over. Bin had arranged for us to have the whole of the main floor lest we were disturbed by sounds coming through the paper thin walls and our meals were pure Japanese brought to us by the landlady on all fours.

Our visit to Hong Kong was organised by an extraordinary female Poobah, Mrs Susan Yuan, born on the mainland, married to the pre-revolutionary head of the Chinese electricity supply industry, who had trained at Metropolitan Vickers, Manchester, and had therefore ordered only Metrovic equipment; she had become in turn secretary or director of almost every Hong Kong industrial organisation, her role as our host being Director of the Hong Kong Design Council, clearly a well heeled body for she was able to put us up for a week at the Mandarin Hotel, from which we seemed ever after to get Christmas wishes. Sir Misha Black was also staying there a few floors above us. He and I were invited to speak at the inaugural dinner of the Hong Kong Designers' Association held in the other great hotel, the Peninsular. By coincidence my cousin, Sir Patrick Reilly, happened to be in Hong Kong leading a trade mission as President of the London Chamber of Commerce and he and I seemed to get alternate billing (Sir Patrick and Sir Paul) in the English language press, though I think I was the only Reilly to be interviewed on the Hong Kong TV and also, I believe, to have a private lunch with the Governor, Sir Murray MacLehose. Two things made our visit to Hong Kong worth recalling; first a gathering of Hong Kong polytechnic students addressed first by me and then by Kenji Ekuan, my Japanese friend who, apart from being a Buddhist monk, was Japan's leading industrial designer, an extraordinary feat really because at that time Kenji spoke almost no English and certainly no Chinese yet he managed to convey his meaning: he talked about design and density or the influence on design of crowded living. And secondly, our meeting the Palmers, Gladys, a Hungarian artist journalist who interviewed and drew Annette, and Simon, a Swire executive, who sailed a splendid junk and took us with great skill through the packed waters of Aberdeen; they later moved to San Francisco, but kept a small house at Fairlight, Sussex and remained in touch with us.

On to New Zealand, flying first class thanks to the generosity of my surviving aunt and stopping for short spells at Darwin, where we saw our first Australian shorts and bare knees, and Sydney, where I had to give a press conference and mentioned Prince Philip and one of our Design Council Awards, a lavatory seat, which appeared in every paper under the sun to judge by the pile of press cuttings on my desk when I got home. New Zealand was a delight, our hosts, Mr and Mrs Geoffrey Nees the most charming of couples, his design organisation, carefully modelled on ours in London, a friendly haven and Wellington a city that recalled for me Bournemouth of fifty years back. We had two weeks in the country, flying everywhere, down to the snows of Mt Cook and the peaceful lake of Wakatipu at Queenstown in the South Island and up to the Bay of Islands in the far north. On this last lap we climbed into a tiny aeroplane to find Peter Calvocoressi and Jim Rose of Penguin Books already installed. Next morning we took off for Brisbane in a DC10, unaware of the shortcomings of that plane, for we ran into a major thunderstorm which blacked out the city and airport; we had what Australians call a real 'white knuckle' landing. Having got off lightly in New Zealand with only two lectures in two weeks I did a full stint in Australia with a speech or two in every city except Canberra, though there was near disaster in Melbourne for the night before I was to address an audience of VIPs, including the Prime Minister, I dropped my teeth on the marble floor of our bathroom (we were in a magnificent old Edwardian hotel) and smashed them. After spending most of the night looking through telephone and other reference books I was lucky enough to find a dental clinic open next morning and able to effect repairs which have lasted ever since. Our tour of Australia was organised by the Australian Design Council which had units in every city, but which shortly afterwards was faced with dissolution through Government economies. It survived by the skin of its teeth, partly perhaps through my having sat next to Rupert Murdoch at a dinner in London; I begged him to speak with Prime Minister Fraser, lest Australia should forever be dependent on imported designs.

Our first visit to South Africa was at the invitation of Shell. I had stipulated that I should be enabled to address a coloured audience and that was agreed. We sailed in the *Pretoria Castle* on one of her last voyages, indeed on one of the last voyages of the Union Castle Line. One bonus of the trip was the day we spent on St Helena, that remarkable mountain rising out of the south Atlantic, tropical at sea level, temperate at the top and at the very top French with the Tricolor flying, the Longwood estate having apparently been presented by Britain to Napoleon's country. The upper reaches of St Helena were very English, like Somerset, with small fields and good Georgian houses. To get there one drove in prewar open cars all worth their weight in gold as veterans. The little church of Jamestown at the foot of the mountain was filled with sad memorials to young Englishmen returning from India in the days of sail and early steam.

South Africa was all that we had heard of it, apartheid in full swing, blue skies and black servants, very beautiful for the whites, deadly, one imagined, for the blacks. I was lucky to meet and to spend some time with the courageous editor of the *Rand Daily Mail* who told me that he would continue to publish his criticisms of the regime until arrested; he expected to have his passport seized, which duly happened before his arrest. He doubted whether I would be given an opportunity to address a coloured audience, a doubt which worried me increasingly as the days went by. I had spoken in Cape Town, Johannesburg,

Pretoria, where the Minister of Finance took the chair, and Durban, my last port of call, but never a coloured face in the audience. Our Shell Pty guide in Natal understood my reluctance to return home without having spoken to a coloured audience and somehow arranged a very early morning expedition to an Indian university outside Durban where I had the best informed audience of the whole tour. Our Natal guide was Ivan Hattingh, who shortly thereafter escaped to Britain where he fell on his feet thanks in the first place to my wife's intervention with the design organisation, Pentagram, one of whose partners was originally South African. Of course, were one able to close one's eyes to the horrors of the regime, South Africa had its enchantments—the lovely farms in the Cape, the train journey across the Kalahari desert, the government offices in Pretoria, Mrs Michaelis's pictures, but above all Kruger National Park where we saw nearly thirty species of wild animals in two days.

Canada was memorable for a transcontinental train journey, three days of wonderful travel, day one through forest and lakes, day two through the endless prairies, day three through the Rockies, with Vancouver and Victoria Island to finish off. In Vancouver we attended a convocation at Simon Fraser University accompanied by the architect, Arthur Erickson, while on Victoria Island we put the clock back and lunched with the VC Lieutenant Governor in his very English, very Victorian mansion. We met two expatriate English designers in Vancouver, one of whom, Ralph Gillett, drove us out to his homestead on Victoria Island and with the other of whom, Warnett Kennedy, I took part in a television programme; he had acquired a great following as a broadcaster.

Before our train journey I had had the pleasure of opening, in French and English, the Design Centre in Montreal. On another visit to Canada we looked in at the Design Centre in Toronto accompanied by Mrs Sonja Bata, whose husband Tom obviously had great influence with an airline which, though fully booked, nonetheless carried us to New York.

I have lost count of our transatlantic visits, but for anyone interested in design, trips to the USA are essential, particularly to the Museum of Modern Art. I was, though, pleased on two occasions to be able to contribute to the development of design in the USA. On the first occasion I was asked to speak to the annual convention of the Industrial Designers Society of America (IDSA) in Kentucky, where I was for some reason commissioned a Kentucky Colonel. While there I discovered IDSA was short of funds and would greatly welcome some help from the US Government. As I was planning to spend a couple of nights in Washington on my way home staying in Georgetown with Michael Straight, at that time Deputy Chairman of the National Endowment for the Arts, I said I would see what could be done. Michael, after asking me to speak to his NEA staff about the support given by the British Government to the Council of Industrial Design in London, jumped at the idea, which he asked me to put next day to his chairman, Nancy Hanks. She responded warmly and promised an annual NEA subsidy to IDSA; this pleased my old friend, Arthur Pulos, who had arranged my trip to Kentucky. My second contribution to design in America was a rather good speech I made in Washington to the second Federal Design Assembly, a gathering of senior public servants and ministers, in which I demonstrated with slides the influence of the Design Council on their opposite numbers in Britain.

From Washington we went to California for a state-wide promotion of British Design in the Broadway chain of stores, with the Hon. Sir Peter Ramsbotham, our Ambassador, inaugurating the event in Los Angeles, while next day we were driven south to San Diego where I performed the same function in another Broadway store, Annette and I shaking hands with some fifteen hundred account customers, most of whom seemed to be Scottish to judge from their tartans. We were put up in San Diego in the splendid Coronado Inn from where we made expeditions to La Jolla and the famous zoo.

I went on our last two visits to New York as President of the

23. With my Russian opposite number in Moscow, Yuri Soloviev, in 1964

24. Greeting the 2,000,000th visitor to our first exhibition in Moscow in 1964

25. Lord Eccles in The Design Centre for an exhibition of crafts

World Crafts Council staying with Mrs Aileen Vanderbilt Webb, the founder, and taking the chair at a meeting in Greystones, an old Vanderbilt house now belonging to Columbia University. During those few days we had the opportunity of seeing our old Swedish friend, Åke Hampus Huldt, in action as Secretary General of the WCC; and how well he performed. It was also at Greystones that we met Arline Fisch, the very creative American silversmith from San Diego, who has had several exhibitions in London.

Mexico is also a country for anyone interested in design to visit and we were fortunate to go there twice, the first time with an exhibition of British design, the second at the invitation of the Mexican design organisation so that I could speak to a group of industrialists. On this occasion we stayed with Sir John and Lady Galsworthy in the Embassy designed by Eric Bedford. Here I was delighted to find that they were eating off china designed by Richard Guyatt, drinking out of glass from Robert Goodden and using silver and flatware by David Mellor, all of which I knew had been commissioned by the Ministry of Works at the instigation of the Council of Industrial Design. The Galsworthys were very careful of their guests and forbade us to do anything other than breathe oxygen for the whole of our first day, for Mexico City is some seven thousand feet above sea level. On our first visit we were taken by Philip Guilmant out to the great pyramids of Teotihuacan where I took a great number of photographs only to find when I got home that the camera had failed to function. I never expected to return to Mexico and wrote the whole lot off in my mind. On our second visit, Philip Guilmant kindly repeated the expedition, this time the camera functioned properly and we have a good record of those extraordinary structures.

Our return journey from our second visit to Mexico took us into the lap of luxury, thanks to the intervention of David Ogilvy, who had suggested to his client Ted Moscoso, the boss of Puerto Rico, that he could benefit or rather that his economy could benefit from a conversation with the Director of the

British Council of Industrial Design. So we were duly invited and housed in a style fit for an Ogilvy in the top two floors of the Caribe Hilton. In exchange I had to speak to a gathering of Puerto Rican businessmen, among whom was a banker called Guillermo Rodriguez-Benitez who not only lived in a splendid modern house but was building a remarkable collection of calligraphy, the best of letterers in his view being Donald Jackson who, I am proud to say, did my Letters Patent, when I was made a peer. A treasure with which we returned from Puerto Rico was a bowl by the potter Jaime Suarez, who took us under his wing, introduced us to his family of craftsmen and showed us the old town of San Juan. He was a friend of Oswaldo Toro the architect whose report following a visit to the Design Centre in London, had set people thinking of establishing something similar in Puerto Rico. I do not know what came of the project but we shall always be grateful for five very comfortable days among very hospitable people, being sung to sleep each night by the chorus of singing tree frogs, which strangely remain silent when taken to adjacent islands.

8

Scandinavia and Italy

I spent my fiftieth and sixtieth birthdays in Sweden and both times was stood a splendid party by my Swedish friends, for the Swedes make much of such occasions, particularly when Åke Huldt and Astrid Sampe are involved, as they are the best of all party givers. For my fiftieth birthday I, not knowing what was in store, was simply told to bring a dinner jacket and turn up at 8 p.m. at Svindersvik, a charming eighteenth-century pavilion on an island near Stockholm, which had been built by a Vasa king for a party of his own and rarely used since. When I got there I found myself to be the centre of candle-lit attention with speech after speech in my honour and each speaker presenting me with a gift of glass, ceramics or a book, but not until we had eaten a feast of cold fish washed down with aquavit; the speeches began with the meat, my own in reply being, I recall, far short of what such an occasion demanded. I don't know how my friends managed to get access to the royal pavilion, but perhaps Count Sigvard Bernadotte, the silver-smith son of the Swedish King, may have had a hand in it for he was certainly present. The moving spirit, however, was Åke Hampus Huldt, the then rector of the Swedish equivalent of our own Royal College of Art, who had formerly been Director of the Svenskaslöjdforeningen, the Swedish equivalent of our Council of Industrial Design. He was also at that time running the Swedish Design Centre in Valhallavägen, the most beautiful, elegant display of Swedish design imaginable, which I had to admit made ours in London look by comparison like a bit of a trollop—not inappropriately perhaps for a centre only a long stone's throw from Piccadilly Circus. The Swedish centre called Svensk Form Design Centre however did not survive; it was financed largely by the generosity of its chairman, Mr Rudolph Kalderen, the head of the great and then glamorous store Nordiska Kompaniet or NK as it was everywhere known; when he retired NK somehow lost interest in design and the Swedish Design Centre folded. But while it was in being it set the highest standards of selection and display. I was very proud to be invited once to stage a British display there, which we did without too much loss of face.

My sixtieth birthday started at Tilbury for, thanks to Astrid Sampe, Annette and I were given the best cabin on board a Swedish Lloyd ship which she had designed, and were greeted on arrival with a bottle of champagne in a bucket of ice. We had with us a painting by Einar Forseth, which he had given to my father; it was his final cartoon for the great wall of the Stockholm town hall's golden mosaic room. I had always felt it to be a piece of archival material that should return to Stockholm. Einar was equally firm that it should stay in England. We came to a compromise: that I should offer it to the British Embassy in Stockholm, thereby satisfying both parties. The British Ambassador, Sir Guy Millard, was not only willing to receive it, but invited us to stay with him and suggested giving a party at which Einar and I should be the guests of honour. I therefore took the painting to Alfred Hecht to have it reframed and inscribed and very handsome it looked when he had finished with it. I hope it still hangs in the Embassy to stimulate conversation.

The next day we boarded the ferry to Helsinki, Annette and I finding ourselves again in the best cabin. We were joined on board by parties of our friends from Norway and Denmark and of course Sweden—a group of some thirty people. Åke Huldt had arranged it all, including a private dining room, a specially composed song in honour of the Reillys, a magnificent gift of four aquavit glasses from each Scandinavian country, every piece carrying an engraved double R and all packed into a splendid transparent box also carrying the double R—this last being Huldt's own contribution—and then for me four large bottles of schnapps, one from each country in a quartered basket. On returning to England I declared the four bottles and was wished a happy birthday by the customs officer. When we got to Helsinki we were met by our Finnish friends, taken to see the fine underground church, and then to Hvitträsk, the splendid Eliel Saarinen house which makes any lover of Charles Rennie Mackintosh feel quite at home. An excellent lunch was followed by speeches, mine being a bit better than usual. We returned by the same ferry that evening with a champagne dinner given to the whole party by Mrs Maire Gullichsen, whose husband had commissioned the young Alvar Aalto to design the famous Villa Mairea. We were lucky enough to spend the night there in 1981; we slept in an Edwardian building, but ate in Aalto's, surrounded by Maire Gullichsen's fabulous collection of modern art.

We were not able to get to Scandinavia for my seventieth birthday, but instead they sent me a very welcome, carefully printed greeting with the following inscription: 'In admiration for his great contribution to the development of British Design; in recognition of his inspiring role in the international promotion of good design; and in grateful appreciation of the friendship, interest and encouragement he has offered his Scandinavian colleagues'. It was signed by the Danish Design Council, the Finnish Society of Crafts and Design, the Finnish Designers' Guild Ornamo, the Norwegian Society of Arts and Crafts and Industrial Design, and the Swedish Society for Industrial Design. There followed the names of some thirty-six Scandinavian designers most of whom had attended my two birthday parties and all of whom had over the years become great friends. Alongside the printed text they had inserted a delightful pen and ink drawing of the Eros statue in Piccadilly Circus by Ebbe Sadolin, the Danish artist with whom we had spent a holiday many years before in Switzerland. The instigator of this generous gesture was once more Åke Huldt, a key figure in our life, who from the early 1950s had tutored our appreciation of Swedish design and who in turn had accepted my invitation in 1966 to stage an excellent exhibition in our Design Centre. This had coincided with his award of an Honorary CBE and I was able to read a telegram from the British Ambassador in Stockholm announcing the award at the opening ceremony in London, thereby repaying to some extent my enormous debt to Swedish design.

Sweden and Italy were the two countries that excelled in design. It was said in those days that the Swedes adopted a democratic approach in their designing, keeping their solutions generally acceptable, while the Italians struck out as individuals, making theirs primarily headline catchers. There is still some truth in this for the Swedes continue to cling to natural materials, the Italians to metal and plastics, the Swedes to quiet, humane forms, the Italians to noisy, exciting ones. Throughout the fifties and sixties there was held in Milan every three years the Milan Triennale, an international exhibition at which every country showed its best in design and at which reputations were made. It was in Milan that the world first realised that Finland was out in front with names like Wirkkala and Franck in the lead, but that Sweden was close behind with Huldt and Sampe and others catching up. The Italians of course excelled for it was their exhibition; they had names like Ponti, Zanuso, Scarpa and Albini, Vignelli and Sottsass (who was later to launch his Memphis range of furniture). Britain was represented in 1951 by Robin and Lucienne Day and their employers, Leslie and Rosamind Julius of Hille, and very well they did. The Council of Industrial Design was fully occupied at that time with the Festival of Britain, but would have wished to take part, as indeed it tried to do three years later without success; the Board of Trade was not willing to find the funds. It was not until David Eccles was President of the Board of Trade and we wanted to show a fully equipped school that we got nearer our goal. He listened sympathetically, but had to tell us that it would be up to the Ministry of Education to find the money; nonetheless he would write to the Minister urging him to do so. That was one of his last letters from the Board of Trade for the Government was reshuffled and he became Minister of Education, thus reading his own letter and happily acting upon it. In the result Britain came out on top, winning the Milan Triennale's highest award.

Another Italian award won by Britain was the Compasso d'Oro which was given to the Council of Industrial Design in 1959. This annual award was created by La Rinascente, the large Milanese department store, which in the following year mounted a display of the Design Centre Awards backed up by stock for sale; at the same time they commissioned from Michael Farr, former editor of *Design* magazine, an excellent account of the work of the Council which they published in Italian and English and which was the best record to date of the Council's achievements. I went to Milan in November 1960 to receive the Golden Compass from Sir Ashley Clarke, the British Ambassador, in the presence of Count Aldo Borletti, the President of La Rinascente, for it put the COID ahead of all its rivals. It also made the Council a familiar institution to many Italian designers, so that we could, without too much difficulty, organise tours for British designers of Italian studios and factories. It was through one of these tours that we first made contact with Olivetti, a relationship which developed well at home through the presence in Olivetti's London office of David Maroni, their director of public relations, with whom Annette and I had a splendid journey round Italy visiting Olivetti plants and offices.

9

Royal Family

The most helpful person to the Design Council throughout my time as director was unquestionably the Duke of Edinburgh. He first came into contact with the old Council of Industrial Design in 1953, when he came to see our exhibition of selected Coronation Souvenirs. Then in 1956 he came to open the Design Centre making a speech that was so good that it went round the world, getting the Centre off to a marvellous start. In 1956 he first came to the Centre to present the Design Centre Awards, thus starting an annual event which he continued for over thirty years. I first met him when in 1959 I had to take Gordon Russell's place and go to Buckingham Palace to hear his admirable suggestion that we should make more of his annual presentation of our awards by holding the meeting away from the Design Centre; he suggested our choosing each year a building of modern architectural distinction, one year in London, the next elsewhere; and our always inviting an audience of distinguished industrialists, people we wished to impress. So began a series of presentations in a series of splendid venues, starting in the Royal College of Art and including the *QEII*, Concorde, the Royal Mint and the National Film Theatre. At each event the Duke made a speech, extolling the importance of good design, and each speech was better than its predecessor.

One's first visit to Buckingham Palace is, I suppose, always something of an ordeal, so magnificent are the furnishings, so thick the carpets, so interesting the pictures and so polite the uniformed staff. On my first visit I was accompanied into the Duke's office, recently remodelled by Sir Hugh Casson, by

General Sir Frederick Browning, who sat discreetly behind my back taking notes. I was glad he was there for he got up when it was time to go. My next visit, still with the General present, was to discuss Prince Philip's suggestion that he should give his own award 'for elegance'. We had some doubt about the wisdom of 'elegance', but I felt happier when the Prince talked about an elegant solution to a problem and much happier when the first award went to a refrigerator. This prize was the occasion for a further annual visit from the Duke of Edinburgh, for he came to the Design Centre to take the chair of his committee—two men, two women—and in the early years he would accept our invitation to lunch after a morning's work. At one of these lunches he told me that he thought he was the luckiest man in the world. I asked why. He replied because he could meet anyone of interest. I thought then of the fantastic range of his interests and of the speed with which he mastered any subject.

My third visit to Buckingham Palace came about at the end of an extraordinary sequence of events, which began with the wedding of Princess Margaret. There was much press speculation about what her husband, Antony Armstrong Jones, would do. Most papers seemed to think he would go to the Arts Council; the *Observer* opted for the Council of Industrial Design, which sent shivers down my spine, for not everyone spoke well of him. For the week beginning 24 October 1960 I was called to jury service, starting at 9.30 am in the South London courts at Newington Causeway. On the Wednesday I was summoned to the Treasury to see Sir Norman Brook. I asked my secretary to get me off, which she was unable to do, so I told her it would have to be an early morning meeting. It was fixed for 8 am on the Friday. When I turned up I found Sir Richard Powell, Permanent Secretary of the Board of Trade, and Sir Rodney Harris of the Treasury, waiting outside Sir Norman's room. Sir Richard just had time to tell me that we were going to discuss Armstrong Jones before we were ushered in. Sir Norman came straight to the point by asking me how I would react to having Armstrong Jones join my staff. I thought fast and said I would object for three reasons. First that ours was a very small organisation and whoever was the Queen's brother-in-law would certainly rock the boat; second, that as far as I knew he was not interested in modern design; and third that I would find it a very poor exchange to swop the Duke of Edinburgh for Antony Armstrong Jones, for I imagined that on Armstrong Jones joining us Prince Philip would pull out. Sir Norman reassured me on my last point saying I could safely leave that with him. Sir Rodney said he felt my second point to be the most difficult. Sir Richard supported my first objection. It was left that I should think about it over the weekend, and keep it all under my hat.

On the following Monday I was called to the Board of Trade to hear from Sir Richard that it now looked to be more a matter of when than of whether, since the Sovereign was taking an interest. On 15th November 1960 I had to give an afternoon lecture in Birmingham and just managed to catch a train back to Paddington, but slipped on the Snow Hill platform and sprained my ankle. I crawled into the nearest carriage which had a reservation ticket on the window in the name of Mrs John Profumo, who got in at the next station. I could not have had a kinder companion. She understood exactly what was wrong with me, took my shoe off, soaked my handkerchief, wrapped it round my ankle and sent for brandies. She even organised a wheelchair to meet me at Paddington and then saw me to my car, which drove me to the casualty department of St George's Hospital. The next morning I dressed in old country clothes and hobbled to work on two sticks. Within the hour I was summoned to Buckingham Palace and taken to Prince Philip's study, this time unaccompanied by the General. Prince Philip sat me on a sofa facing the fireplace and walked up and down a few times and then said, 'I don't know how to begin this.' I said, 'Is it by any chance about Armstrong Jones?' He said it was and asked me how I knew about it. I told him of my talk with the three knights and he replied, 'Good Lord does all the top brass of the Civil Service know about it?' He then asked me what I felt. I stated my same objections, to which he replied that I need not fear that he would pull out for his was a personal interest which he would not give up. The question of Armstrong Jones being too big a fish for our little boat was an administrative matter, which I would have to solve; but he could not comment on the point about his interest in modern design. He said we must find out and picked up the telephone. Armstrong Jones was out but he would telephone me. We then discussed my concern for modern design and he asked me what I thought of his John Nash fire surround. 'Admirable', I said, 'but not for reproduction today,' with which he agreed, though I felt that like many Britons he was not always happy about modern designs.

A few days later Armstrong Jones came on to my phone and asked to come and see me but, 'May I make one thing quite clear? I do not take my opinions from my uncle (Oliver Messel).' That was comforting and I enjoyed meeting him, but there was one more hurdle before he could join us. We had to decide how much to pay him. I went back to Sir Norman Brook for advice. He said we could not pay him anything for any figure would be wrong. If we paid him what he was earning before his marriage—which he later told me was £14,000 per annum, considerably more than I was getting—there would be an outcry since his wife was in receipt of generous public funding; if we paid him much less he would not accept it. So nothing it was and he was really very good value whatever he did for us. We took a lot of trouble drafting a press handout, explaining that he would act as a consultant on our exhibition programme and help with our educational activities, and we fixed his arrival for 23 January 1961, a Monday, hoping thereby to dampen press enthusiasm. But not a bit of it. When I got in that morning the Design Centre was besieged by cameramen; they had climbed onto adjacent roofs to get a view into my office, they were at every window in Haymarket overlooking the Centre; and they were massed on the pavement outside.

When we got to my office Tony gave me a piece of bad news. He told me that he had undertaken a commission for the zoo which he had to finish by a given date and he could therefore not find much time for us. I protested that we had told the press that he would put in a full day's work like anyone else, but he was adamant. We got out of it by saying that he was working for us at home, which deceived nobody. All was well, however, when the Zoo unveiled his aviary, which I had seen one evening at Kensington Palace where I had my first meeting with Princess Margaret; she was helping Tony to make the model of the aviary.

My next visit to Buckingham Palace was at my own request. I wanted Prince Philip's approval for a new form of award to recognise good design management in everything from architecture to print. He was very receptive, but suggested that we, the Council of Industrial Design, should stick to products, and that the new award should be handled by the Royal Society of Arts, of which he was President. This seemed a good idea and one I could sell to the RSA since I was a member of its Council. It was agreed that the Council of Industrial Design should survey the field biannually, should then submit its selection of companies to a joint RSA/COID committee and that up to six companies should be chosen. Prince Philip further suggested that each chairman should speak for not longer than twelve minutes to explain how, why and with what results his company had pursued its policy. Thus every second year the RSA/COID Award for the Management of Design produces texts on this important aspect, which one day will provide useful educational material, particularly since the Duke of Edinburgh's remarks as Chairman are always printed in the RSA journal. This was in fact another example of Prince Philip's gift for enlarging an idea to contribute to a bigger cause. When he put up the idea for his own elegance prize he suggested—and I agreed—that the winner should be asked to design or commission his prize to the value of £200; he should be named one year and receive his award the following one, thus meeting the Duke of Edinburgh twice and thus, hopefully, producing something that would have a future success on the market.

The most exciting of our award ceremonies was my last one in 1977. We chose the new theatre at Inverness as the venue, but planned a full day's outing by taking the night train up, decanting into the delightful cross-Scotland train from Inverness to Kyle of Lochalsh where we embarked on a steamer to take us to see the largest concrete structure ever made: the Howard Doris oil platform being built at Kishorn, a remarkable feat of engineering, almost all of which, alas, was under water, but a good deal of which I had seen on an earlier visit. I recall the dimensions of this vast structure: the base as large as Trafalgar Square, the height that of the Eiffel Tower, the platform at the top as big as Twickenham rugby field. When we saw it on that beautiful May morning only the platform was visible for it had already been towed out to deep water; later on it would be towed round the north of Scotland to its final resting place in the North Sea. At the presentation ceremony Prince Philip made one of his excellent speeches in which, to my astonishment, he referred to me saying:

'Sir Paul Reilly has done more than just make the Council work, he has infused the whole organisation with a wonderful sense of enthusiasm and dedication. He has made its purpose to encourage rather than to lecture, to praise rather than to hector and, full of ideas himself—witness this excursion to the Highlands—he has never been a member of the "not-invented-here" club.'

Tony Armstrong Jones, or Snowdon as he was soon to be, became over the years a close friend of mine. It was not easy to get him to work acceptable hours even though we allowed him to design his own office and of course when he joined *The Sunday Times* we saw even less of him. But he managed some useful industrial tours of Ulster, Wales and Scotland, mostly organised by Dan Johnston, our chief industrial officer. His three Welsh tours were perhaps the most successful not only because he was himself Welsh but because we had a wonderfully enthusiastic Welsh member of our Council, Mervyn T. Jones, who became the first chairman of our Welsh committee. An industrial tour fitted inside a week and involved two or three factory visits every day, with a lunch or dinner for local industrialists and speeches by Mervyn and me and, when he felt more secure on his feet, by Tony. It was interesting for someone like me, who hated speaking, to watch Tony going through the same agonies but gradually overcoming his nerves so that eventually he could get up in the House of Lords and speak without notes. It was also interesting to observe the declining press interest in his tours; at the beginning we were escorted everywhere by journalists and photographers driving with us in convoy and picketing our hotels, but gradually this interest lapsed, though there was no diminution in the enthusiasm of the work forces visited.

Our two Ulster tours were before the troubles began. We stayed at Hillsborough Castle with the governors, Lords Wakehurst and Erskine of Kerrick and very comfortable we were. Prime Minister O'Neill gave a lunch for us at Stormont with Tony on his right and on his left Senator Michael ffrench O'Carroll from Dublin, who was at that time Chairman of the Irish Design Council. The occasion was a small indication of how things might have gone had O'Neill stayed. On our second visit Tony opened an exhibition from London's Design Centre in the Ulster Hall; it was one of our series of 'The Design Centre comes to . . .', exhibitions by which we were able to take the Design Centre round the country. We had a problem returning from Belfast owing to a British Airways strike. Tony was determined to get back to Kensington Palace and so begged a lift from Short Brothers, one of the factories on our list. The managing director, who later joined our Council in London, was most cooperative and offered us his plane and pilot—my first experience of sitting in a cockpit while the plane was brought down at Heathrow; it reminded me of the flight simulator in the British pavilion at the 1958 Brussels Expo.

It was normal for Tony to want to involve Princess Margaret in his work and gratifying that she had no objection, for she had a good eye and had herself had a shot at designing. She once showed me a tea set that she had designed as a gift from the potter concerned. It had a pattern composed of straight lines which fitted well onto the straight sides of the cups, but imagine her concern when the same potter presented her with a wedding present of a bowl also with the same straight lines fitting very ill on its well-rounded sides. Princess Margaret was convinced that we had plenty of work to do. She came frequently to the Design Centre, often officially to open an exhibition and she performed the same ceremony at various of our foreign ventures at British Weeks— at Copenhagen, for instance, or Amsterdam or Paris. At Copenhagen Tony began explaining to me how members of the Royal Family like to give small presents to people who had been helpful but how badly designed they were. Later that evening the British Ambassador, Sir John Henniker-Major, gave a party at the Embassy. In the middle of it he said to me that Princess Margaret was in a small adjacent room and would like to see me. I went in and found her standing in the middle of the room with a small box in her hand. Tony was behind her. She held out the box and said, 'This is for you. Mind you always wear them.' In the box was a pair of gold cuff-links with her cypher engraved on them—an M with a coronet above it. I caught Tony's eye as he winked at me but, though I now understood his earlier conversation, I have done as I was told and have worn the links ever since, thus saving them from being stolen when we were burgled for the third time and every piece of gold in our house was removed.

Before the Amsterdam week Tony suggested that I should write to all Dutch architects and designers of any note inviting them to lunch with my wife and myself at Otterlo to meet Princess Margaret. This I did and we acted as hosts to a distinguished gathering in van de Velde's admirable museum. We tried something else new in Amsterdam, again at Tony's suggestion. He had rightly thought that our exhibition openings needed enlivening so we fixed up a large sort of envelope across the entrance to Berlage's bourse in which we had installed our show. The envelope was stretched on springs behind, a small eye hole had been pierced in the middle and a string for cutting laid across the front. It was fairly disastrous, for cut as she did, the paper would not tear. We had to rend it by hand. However we got a good photo of her nose poking through the eye hole. The Paris exhibition, planned during my cousin's time at our Embassy but opened in Christopher Soames's, was good only in parts—I had a letter of apology from the designers afterwards—but it was backed up by some magnificent entertainment—a great dinner at the British Embassy and a greater one at the Quai D'Orsay, hosted by the French foreign minister, M. Schumann, with Princess Margaret in full beauty. Annette and I were proud to think that we had had her dine with us at home, Annette having cooked a splendid dinner without, I believe, our guest of honour realising it.

In the mid-sixties Annette had to go into hospital for an operation. She was very ill and I nearly lost her. Then two years later she was back again, this time for an operation for cancer. A few days before she was due to come home Princess Margaret telephoned to ask us to dinner. I explained that we would love it if it could be a small party, since Annette was just coming out of hospital. 'Oh, it will be small,' she said, 'just Tony and my sister.' In the event there were three others present, Lord Plunket and Mr and Mrs Dennis Lennon. At dinner Tony asked the Queen whether she would like to visit the Design Centre where we had an exhibition about the *QEII*, that was Dennis Lennon's achievement. She agreed and I just managed to telephone the Centre in time to keep it open. Princess Margaret decided not to come since she had already seen the show when she opened it a few days before. It was the

26. With Bernard Leach and Shoji Hamada of Japan, August 1970

27. Three directors and two chairmen, Lord Caldecote on left, Sir Duncan Oppenheim on right. In the middle Sir Gordon Russell. On his right Keith Grant, my successor

28. Congratulating Dr Åke Huldt on his Hon CBE. On the right Count Sigvard Bernadotte and in the middle Gunnar Hägglöf, the Swedish Ambassador

Queen's second visit to the Centre but the only one of which we got a proper photographic record. 'Please don't be photographed looking interested,' said Princess Margaret. 'Why not?' said the Queen. 'Because it makes you look so grim,' replied her sister. On Her Majesty's first visit Tony asked me whether we might give her a present. I agreed. Tony said she could choose anything there; she turned to me for confirmation, saying 'Carpets for instance?' I had visions of our recarpeting Buckingham Palace, but she said she must go round again and to my relief settled for a coffee set. It was on that visit that Princess Margaret was discovered smoking a cigarette through her long holder and sitting cross-legged on one of our loos. 'What on earth are you doing?' said the Queen. 'Testing for comfort, Ma'am,' replied the Princess.

I had had a little to do with the design of the QEII and the appointment of Dennis Lennon and James Gardner, for to start with there were rumours that a woman famous for her chintzy interiors was to be employed. I wrote to the Chairman of Cunard and protested that the ship should really be a flag bearer for modern British design. I offered to show him some slides of the kind of work I had in mind. He sent his naval architect to see them and he was impressed. They chose Dennis Lennon to oversee the interior and James Gardner to do the exterior silhouette, but one day when the great ship was well advanced I had a call from James Gardner begging my help over the funnel which the Cunard company wanted to have painted in the familiar red and black of the earlier *Queens*. I went to Hampstead to see the two schemes, was convinced by James's and Dennis's arguments, and promised to do what I could. I rang Tony Snowdon who said he would not intervene, but suggested my talking with Princess Margaret who was going to Sandringham, where she would meet Prince Philip. I spoke with her, she agreed to seek Prince Philip's help, took my telephone number, said she would ask him to telephone me after dinner and went off to Sandringham. I waited on tenterhooks by my telephone. The call came through around eleven o'clock. Prince Philip asked me rather gruffly what this was all about. I tried to explain. He said his sympathies were with the Cunard people, for he liked shipping lines' loyalties to their traditional colouring, but he would nonetheless have a word with his old friend Sir Basil Smallpiece, the new Cunard chairman. In the event James Gardner's scheme went through unaltered, and very fine it looked when we went to Southampton to hold our awards ceremony on board, a ceremony which scored two firsts: the ship and the train from Waterloo, for British Rail had managed to provide us with the first of their inter-city trains, specially brought round London from Euston or King's Cross.

One thing I always enjoyed about Snowdon was the way he seized his opportunities, acting on the spur of the moment, as when we met one day at a luncheon in Quaglinos. It was shortly before Christmas and he asked me after lunch whether I knew the Queen Mother. I did not so he said that we should drive in his jeep to call on her and see if she would come to the Design Centre. We drove to Clarence House and while waiting for the Queen Mother I telephoned my secretary to warn her and to ask her to get a bottle of champagne. The Queen Mother clearly liked Tony and cheerfully climbed into the jeep or land-rover while I got into the back. It was a strange little party going down the Mall, round Trafalgar Square and into Oxendon Street and then steeply down to the basement where Tony parked. We then went on foot to the basement door of the Design Centre and knocked loudly. Eventually a doorman opened it and began expostulating that that was not the way in. He then saw me and let us in, but I am sure he did not recognise the Queen Mother. Indeed not many people did recognise her as we went up through three floors of the exhibition. The champagne was warm but welcome. We talked of a previous visitor, a duchess, to whom we had also offered a drink. 'Oh dear,' said the Queen Mother, 'not my favourite woman. I am always afraid of her.' Several years later the Queen Mother paid another visit to the Centre when we had an exhibition of modern things, both manufactured and handmade, which could make good official presents for ministers or for royalty. It was a successful little show put on jointly by the Design Council and the Crafts Advisory Committee of which I was at the time chief executive.

Our Welsh connection developed well with the renting of space near the middle of Cardiff for an office and a showroom and the engagement of Peter Cambridge as head of the office. The chairman of our Wales committee at the time was called Oxford, which seemed appropriate. We were of course keen to win Prince Charles's interest. He had, on his father's instructions, already visited the Design Centre, so he knew a little of what we did and was willing to lend his name, following his investiture, to our efforts in Wales. He agreed to our organising an annual competition for Welsh-made products to receive a Tarian or shield of excellence and he came to Cardiff to present them. On that first occasion I was sitting on his right-hand side and had a good view of him preparing his speech. My speech of thanks was of course properly typed out and in my pocket. His was jotted down on the back of an envelope, which started off spotless, the last words appearing as he rose to speak.

At my previous meeting in the Design Centre with the Prince of Wales we had spoken of the great scope for female employment in engineering. I believe it was Women Engineers' Year or some such title and I recall Dr Hugh Conway joining the discussion. A few months later my wife and I were invited to Windsor Castle for supper; the guest of honour was the Queen of Holland. We stopped on the way for dinner at Bray with Milner Gray and his wife and the four of us all went on to Windsor together. The Queen was receiving her guests with Prince Philip at the top of the stairs. Prince Philip said to me that he was afraid there was nothing modern for me to look at—a statement also made to me by Lord George-Brown when we met in the House of Lords. Prince Philip then handed me on to Prince Charles who asked me how my recruitment of female engineers was coming along, and I thought how fortunate he was not only to be such an easy speaker but also to have such a good memory.

Our next visit to Windsor Castle started with a telephone call from Admiral Sir Peter Ashmore saying that, although Her Majesty was in the antipodes on board the *Britannia*, he had had a signal instructing him to invite my wife and me to Windsor Castle 'to sup and sleep'. He offered me two dates in April, one of which was impossible because I would be in Moscow. The second date meant only getting out of a dinner so we were left eagerly anticipating our first night at Windsor. Sir Peter had told me that there would be a senior politician among the guests; he said, 'Let's see who it will be. Oh, not bad; it will be the Prime Minister.' I was glad of that for I had met Jim Callaghan only rarely since the days in the late 1940s when we used to meet fairly regularly for lunch at PEP, when PEP ran a club restaurant in Old Queen Street. In due course further information arrived about visiting Windsor Castle; one piece which, alas, I declined because he lived nearby, was an invitation for my driver to spend the night somewhere in the castle. At last the day arrived. We had to be at Windsor by 6.45 p.m., but so early were we that we drove round and round the town to eat up the minutes, arriving eventually on the dot; and there on the steps of the royal entrance we saw with relief the smiling face of Henriette, Lady Abel Smith, one of the Queen's ladies-in-waiting whom we had got to know, when Alex, her husband, and I were lecturing for the British National Export Council as an introduction to the British Weeks in European capitals. She told us that we had been given rooms in the Edward III Tower which Hugh Casson had designed many years before. We just had time to enjoy our four rooms and their 'contemporary' furniture before we were fetched by a young courtier and taken down a spiral staircase and along a great corridor flanked by portraits to a pleasant gilded drawing room where Prince Philip and Princess Margaret were standing in for the Queen who was closeted with the Prime Minister. They arrived within minutes, accompanied by a number of corgis, and we all settled down to some pre-dinner drinking, but not for long since we had to get back to our rooms to change, for which we had twenty minutes. The Admiral led us out and along the great corridor, but half-way down I heard him say, 'Prime Minister now you've gone too far,' and Jim Callaghan turned back. There were about thirty at table, I with Mrs Callaghan on my left and the wife of the Algerian Ambassador on my right. After dinner we were shown some of the State Rooms and then taken to the Library, where the librarian had sorted out various treasures, each aimed at one or other of the guests. For me he had selected some excellent architectural drawings by King George III and one or two original Joseph Nash views of the interior of the Crystal Palace. My wife found herself looking through albums of royal family photographs with Prince Philip helping to identify the faces. Later we returned to another drawing room for drinks and talk until bed-time at 1.15 a.m. We said goodbye to our hosts before retiring.

I saw them both on a splendid occasion in Westminster Abbey—their Silver Wedding service—at which I found myself surprisingly in the front row just outside the chancel from where I got a marvellous view of all the courtiers and uniforms. Prince Philip recognized me as the royal couple walked out of the Abbey. I got no sight of them at St Paul's where the Jubilee service was held, because our seats were in one of the aisles, Annette's being right on top of a grille giving onto the crypt from which she got a stream of cold air up her skirt. This made her want to go to the lavatory, which she found at the far end of our aisle; it was reserved for priests but she used it.

After my first lunch at Buckingham Palace, at which Basil Spence was the only guest I knew, I got to know Lord Plunket, a great friend of the Queen and a member of her household; he asked me if I could help him find a modern coffee set for the Queen to give to a visiting potentate. I gladly agreed and collected a large number of coffee pots which Plunket came round to Haymarket to see. He chose six to show the Queen who chose one. Plunket also told me that the Queen would like to get to know more architects and designers whom she could ask to her lunch parties and could I provide some names and addresses. This I also did and was glad to see their names in the lists published in *The Times*. I was asked for a second batch which included the name of a very noisy friend who had broken up more than one of our own dinner parties. He was in due course listed and spoke afterwards with great enthusiasm about the lunch, but could not imagine why he had been invited. I never told him.

10

More Travel

Our Hungarian friends living in England had told me enthusiastically about the way of life in Hungary, describing Budapest as if it were Vienna; but not a bit of it, at least when we were there. Fortunately we were staying with Sir Alex and Lady Morley at the British Embassy so we were comfortable, but the city as a whole was just another East European disaster, with nothing in the shops to attract a Western eye. Our British exhibition therefore got off to a good start, rendered all the better by our showing for the first time in Eastern Europe an excellent film produced by the Central Office of Information built around things that had been shown in the Design Centre; and for the first time I was able to conduct a seminar for Hungarian students of design who crowded round with hundreds of questions. Like their contemporaries in Yugoslavia and in Leningrad what they most wanted to know was whether an English designer was free to create what he wanted or had to do as he was told.

Prominent among the countries which sought help in establishing something similar to the Design Council was Israel. Annette and I went there twice, the first time as guests of the Israeli Government, the second time when on holiday in Cyprus, but on both occasions we owed a great deal to Sir John Barnes the British Ambassador in Tel Aviv. We flew out EL AL, stayed a few days in the Tel Aviv Hilton, visited Mrs Ruth Dayan in her boldly-conceived craft shop, explored Old Jaffa and met Frank and Batya Meisler, he being one of the very few Israelis we came across who had been educated in Manchester; he is now a successful designer and sculptor, making all manner of small objects for Batya to sell. The journey by car to Jerusalem took us up the road that had been fought over in 1948; it was still lined by burnt-out, rusting relics of military hardware. Our hotel in Jerusalem was the oddly-named American Colony, a splendid patrician building of Turkish ancestry built round a courtyard. It was owned by an American couple, the wife having been at Oxford with me, when she taught me to dance in Michael Foot's large room in Wadham. She was at that time called Valerie Richmond, her first husband having been James Mason, the film actor. It was good to have an old friend running the place because within a few days first I and then Annette went down with a virulent 'flu. Annette was cared for by an old Arab who brought large sponges and towels dipped in vinegar which he placed on her stomach, the chill from these ice-cold dressings serving to reduce her fever. To reduce mine I drank tea without milk and a great amount of rice water. We both managed to be on our feet on Christmas Eve and went to Bethlehem, but the most interesting excursion was through the mountains of Moab to Jericho and the Dead Sea. It was extraordinary to pass from mid-winter to midsummer and back in one day and quite enough to bring on Annette's flu. In spite of our wasted days in bed we managed to do our duty by our hosts, calling upon the leading art school in Jerusalem, the Bezalel School, visiting their Department of Industry to explain the funding and working of the COID in London and lecturing to an audience convened by George Wertheim, the then director of their institute. We also managed to visit the Knesset seeing, to our delight, Mr Ben Gurion in full flood of oratory; and finally, before returning home, we flew down to Eilat, passing over the greening of the Negev desert and eventually over King Solomon's mines. From Eilat we spent an hour in a glass-bottomed boat enjoying the beauty of the underwater world. George Wertheim did us one further kindness; he arranged for us to fly back first class, again by EL AL, but I was unable to enjoy it because as we packed to go my 'flu returned. I got home and went to bed.

29. Flowers and friendship in Helsinki. On my right Åke Huldt, on my left Yuri Soloviev and Kenji Ekuan

30. With Annette in the early seventies in The Design Centre

31. In Armenia with a coptic priest and Yuri Soloviev

32. Lighting candles with Yuri Soloviev in an ancient church near Tiblisi, Georgia

33. With Annette and Lord Snowdon in Stockholm
34. Explaining Design Index to HRH The Duke of Kent

Two and a half years later we were in Cyprus, holidaying in the journalist Diana Pollock's house near Kyrenia. Our holiday coincided with the Tel Aviv International Fair at which the Design Council had a stand. Sir John Barnes invited us to come over for four days to see it and to stay with him and his wife, Cynthia, at his Embassy. We found an Italian ship to take us from Larnaka to Haifa, where we were to be met for a car tour of Northern Israel. When boarding the ship we went out with half a dozen passengers in a small open boat. I noticed that one of the passengers was a young Japanese student wearing a headband and carrying a black cello case. He went to sit opposite to us so, remembering the recent terrorist activity in Israel by a party of young Japanese, I went across to sit by him in case he had a gun in the cello case. If he were to try anything I would have been in a good position to foil him. All was well, but we learned that when he tried to land at Haifa the Israelis took the same view of him, and opened the cello case, finding it full of terrorist revolutionary literature. He was forbidden access and was returned to the ship whose next port of call would be Genoa.

Next morning we went to the British Pavilion at the Trade Fair, after which we attended a lunch given by the Anglo/Israel Chamber of Commerce at which I had to speak. The following morning entailed a lecture to members of the Israel Design Institute and then a lunch given by John Barnes for three Israelis, including Mr Shimon Peres, then Minister of Transport, later Prime Minister, an amusing talkative man. The afternoon was taken up by the Queen's birthday party at which all the top Israeli brass was present. In preparation for this event my wife and the Barnes's other house guest, Michael Sieff had hoovered the Embassy, so difficult was it to find any staff for ordinary domestic work.

We returned to Cyprus by air next day after being seen off by John and Cynthia Barnes. John stood us Bloody Marys at the airport and we drank to Israel. We next saw the Barneses in Holland when he was Ambassador in The Hague still wearing his multi-coloured ties. They had invited us over for their elder daughter's wedding which was carried out in full traditional Dutch fashion with two carriages, one black, the other, in which the bride travelled, white with white horses. We returned to Holland once more before John's retirement for an exhibition of British design and an Anglo-Dutch symposium at which Roy Worskett and I spoke for Britain with John Barnes in the chair. It happened that another visitor to the British Embassy in The Hague was Roy Jenkins, in good talkative form.

We got back to Cyprus in time to accept an invitation from His Beatitude the President Makarios for morning coffee in his palace; this had obviously once been the British Governor's house because our royal coat of arms still dominated his sitting room. He was interested to learn that Annette's brother Nigel had been his military guardian when we had exiled him to the Seychelles; he bore Britain no ill will for this; indeed, rather the reverse for he told us that he had tried to buy the house in which he had been held, but could raise only £10,000 which was not enough. We spoke also of new building on Cyprus and I begged him to forbid tower blocks; he agreed, but was less enthusiastic about my suggestion that he should slap a heavy tax on the Coca-Cola signs throughout the island, the revenue to pay for archaeological exploration; he replied that there were not enough archaeologists in the world to dig all the sites in Cyprus for wherever one put a spade in the ground one unearthed a Greek or Roman relic.

Our last trip behind the Iron Curtain was to Bulgaria where our host was Minko Hassimsky, the Director of the Bulgarian Institute of Industrial Design. The excuse was the staging of yet one more excellent exhibition of British Design. Our visit started with a couple of nights at the rather grand British Embassy where we were guests of Mr and Mrs (now Sir Edwin and Lady) Bolland. They gave an excellent dinner party for us to meet the Bulgarians into whose hands they would deliver us in two days time, when we were taken to the Sofia Hotel, a modern sort of building on a curve facing the cathedral. They also provided us with a good little interpreter called Nina who waited upon us for the first week, her place being taken by an astonishingly handsome philologist called Dimiter Stepanov for the second week. During that first week we stayed in or near Sofia, visiting restaurants and sites nearby, including the Bulgarian version of Moscow's great store GUM, where once more we were able to judge the gap between East and West. We also managed a design symposium with Kenneth Grange, Bruce Archer, Geoffrey Constable and myself speaking and Nina struggling to translate. One wondered what the docile audience got out of it.

Next day we set off on a week-long motor tour of Bulgaria with Hassimsky and Stepanov and a driver. Annette, who gets car sick, sat in front. Our first stop was Koprivstica, a charming, mainly wooden village with a little wooden inn, where we drank a lot of slivovitz; the meal started with a Shopska salad, that is chopped herbs, tomatoes, cucumber and hard white sheep's cheese piled on top. This was the first course of every meal, but it went well with Slivovitz. The drive through Bulgaria was both ravishing and distressing—ravishing for the frequent beauty of the countryside, for the wild flowers, the acres of roses and mile upon mile of lavender fields; distressing for the squalor of the human habitations, for the callous indifference of the polluting factories and the grotesquely ugly blocks of flats along the Black Sea coast. Fascinating were the archaeological remains like the Kazanlak tomb and the walls of Hissar, but exploration is still in its infancy for the countryside is strewn with *tumuli*, many of which must still contain buried treasures. The wartime discovery of the Kazanlak tomb was such an eye opener and the tomb became such a tourist attraction that the authorities decided to reproduce it nearby, so that only VIPs could see the real thing. Minko had not apparently thought of this, so we spent a long time hanging about while he telephoned Sofia before he got permission for us to don white coats and carpet slippers and go in. It was worth all the waiting to see the astonishing paintings of a fair-skinned woman on a throne linking arms with a dark-skinned man and in support her grooms with saddle horses, while horses and chariots raced each other round the ceiling, the movement at the top of the honey pot contrasting with the stillness of the wall pictures. Our last port of call on the Black Sea was Varna with its vast seaside park; we were to return there many years later when on a Royal Viking cruise.

11

Six Influences

Six bodies contributed greatly to my enjoyment of design: the Royal College of Art; the Royal Society of Arts; the Society of Industrial Artists and Designers; the Royal Institute of British Architects; the British Railways Board; and the International Council of Societies of Industrial Design (ICSID). My first dealings with the RCA were rather strained. The senior common room was in Cromwell Road. Robin Darwin, the principal, had been Education Officer to the Council of Industrial Design, but before my time. He was in full vigour and dominated the assembled company. He asked me one day how on earth I could spend my time on such a boring subject as industrial design, but he was planning to found a professorship of industrial design to which he appointed Misha Black on my recommendation. Another person I introduced into the College was Bruce Archer. I had met him when he was teaching at the Central School of Arts and Crafts of which I was a governor. When I mentioned him to Robin Darwin he was dismissed as 'that dreadful windbag', but I persevered and he was taken on and became in due course Professor of Design Research and Design Education and a much respected figure. He also became an invaluable member of my own Council. When Robin was preparing to retire I tried to infiltrate J. Christopher Jones and mentioned him to Robin, who told me I was mad to consider him or at least that was the departmental view. Again I persevered and brought Jones to lunch with Robin. Fortunately Christopher Cornford and Misha Black joined us and Jones was in good form. After lunch Robin wanted to know more about him and then himself suggested that he should put in for the rectorship; but, alas, Jones had only just accepted the design professorship at the Open University and felt unable to apply.

By this time I was getting on well with Robin, going to stay weekends at Ham where he and Ginette had a rather grand Victorian house, and even having my portrait painted by him—an event which came about more by accident than design. Annette had greatly admired Robin's portrait of Robert Goodden, which she had seen at the Royal Academy and said to Robin one day how much she would like him to paint me. This Robin took to be a commission. He arranged for me to visit John Hedgecoe at the College to have some photographs taken. There I found Robin Darwin and Ruskin Spear and between them a decanter of port; they took it in turns to photograph me in different poses, John Hedgecoe being apparently quite happy to expose hundreds of plates. When the port was gone, we called it a day and I thought no more about it until we were again called to Ham for the weekend. I was told to report next morning to the studio where I sat to Robin for a couple of hours at the end of which the portrait was ready for inspection. It now hangs in our dining room, having first been exhibited at the Royal Academy. Annette was bowled over when the bill came in; she felt better about it after showing a Napoleon Ivy Wedgwood vegetable dish to Arthur Bryan, the Chairman of Wedgwood, who valued it at around what Robin was asking. Robin had given the dish to her when she asked about a collection of pottery on the garage floor; Robin had replied that Ginette had thrown it all out for some reason, even though it had been in daily use by the great Charles Darwin.

By now I was very much part of the RCA Establishment—a member of Council and a Senior Fellow with only an Honorary Doctorate to come, which my friend Lord Esher, Robin's successor, kindly arranged for me, just as several years earlier when he was President of the RIBA he had arranged for me to be made an Hon. FRIBA. Lord Esher's spell as rector coincided with great student unrest, including the occupation of his offices, all of which was very saddening to him for he had set out at the start of his rectorship to court the students and their aspirations. I got involved to some extent for I offered, unsuccessfully as it turned out, to act as intermediary. Lionel Esher's successor, Professor Richard Guyatt, had the difficult tasks of continuing combat with the students coupled with handling increasing financial crises, precipitated to some extent by a critical report by the Visiting Committee, headed by G. B. R. Feilden, who had been a great support to me at the Design Council when I extended its role into the engineering world. My nineteen years on the College Council came to an end with Dick Guyatt's retirement. They had been good years with many friendships among the staff and not a few among the students.

I did not discover until long after he was dead that my father had been a fellow of the Royal Society of Arts, but even without his support I joined it and thanks to Sir Harry Lindsay's intervention became a Life Fellow for only thirty pounds. I was a member of Council from 1959–1962 and from 1963–1970, the break occurring because illness prevented me from attending enough monthly meetings. I was, though, lucky to be re-elected for, although the Council's membership always seemed fairly senile, the RSA was a useful platform for various design activities, some generated by the Society itself, others by my own Council. I gave four or five lectures there and took the chair at several more, earning on the way the Society's Bicentenary Medal. A great advantage was that Prince Philip was President of the Society, so apart from the biannual presentations of the RSA Presidential Awards for Design Management, he kindly took the chair for me on two occasions, one being a review of the Design Council's own awards at which he sought the recipients' views on winning them, the other being a joint gathering of design consultants and management consultants when I hoped that the latter would increasingly employ the former.

The first gong I ever received was the Honorary Fellowship

of the Society of Industrial Artists and Designers. This was in 1959, the year before I became Director of the Council of Industrial Design. It gave me great satisfaction because the SIAD is the professional body of designers and it was, indeed still is, essential that the COID should get on with the SIAD. To ensure this I organised regular meetings between the four or five top members of the Society and my 'heads of divisions' at which we told each other what we had been doing and what we were planning. I was always delighted to be asked to their Minerva Dinners, held in the beautiful Apothecaries' Hall, to which each member invited a businessman of his or her choice and to which the President invited some key figure to speak. I was only very sorry to have to refuse the invitation when it came my way after my retirement, but also after a stroke.

The RIBA bulked very large in my childhood memories for my father was a keen member and gave of his best to the Institute; in return they gave him the Royal Gold Medal for Architecture. He did not come to collect it until after the war when he spoke without notes, falling into the trap of losing his thread and talking for far too long—a lesson that his son took to heart. As my generation began to reach the top I began increasingly to take part in events at the RIBA. I attended lectures and suppers and eventually became chairman of the architectural library, where I had the great pleasure of meeting David Dean, the very talkative librarian, who on his retirement wrote an excellent book on the architecture of the thirties. I knew all the presidents from Lord Holford onwards. Lord Holford cooked us a splendid Christmas dinner the year before he died and regaled us with very funny stories about life in the House of Lords, a fine view of which he had from his bed in St Thomas's Hospital where he died, wondering why fate should take him before his wife, who had been incapacitated for years after a stroke.

A memorable event at the RIBA was the great party given by Michael Manser, the President, to close the 1984 Festival of Architecture. It afforded everyone lucky enough to be there the opportunity to see the splendid exhibition from the drawings collection called 'The Art of Architecture' which had been brilliantly designed by Alan Irvine, Royal Designer for Industry, who as a young man just finishing at the Royal College of Art, came to see me to seek some introductions in Milan, as a result of which he ended up in the offices of BBPR, whose surviving partners were then Enrico Peressuti and Ernesto Rogers. Alan complained to me at that first meeting that the students at the Royal College of Art had almost no contact with their professors and none at all with the principal, a complaint which had a long life at the College.

I suppose that one by-product of my association with the RIBA was Alex Gordon's recommendation of my name as a layman to Lord James of Rusholme, the Chairman of the Royal Fine Art Commission. He accepted me and I was a member for about six years under the secretaryship of Frank Fielden who was succeeded by my friend Sherban Cantacuzino. A few years earlier Sir Desmond Plummer (now Lord Plummer of St Marylebone) asked me to join the Greater London Council Historic Buildings Committee, then under the energetic chairmanship of Lady Lewisham (now Lady Spencer) the secretary being Ashley Barker. This was an admirable non-political institution which attracted keen Greater London councillors like Louis Bondy, Mrs Chaplin and William Bell, who later established the London Heritage Trust; outside membership included John Betjeman, Hugh Casson, Ian Philips and John Summerson. Ashley Barker lectured to the first annual general meeting of the Thurloe and Egerton Association of which I was the first chairman; he spoke with great authority about the development of the London he loved.

The work of the GLC Historic Buildings Committee was of course closely allied to that of the Civic Trust, with which I had many dealings over the years, starting with the very first gathering of architects at which Mr (now Lord) Duncan Sandys outlined his intentions to found a body to defend our heritage. Present were people like J. M. Richards, the then editor of the *Architectural Review*, Frederick Gibberd, Basil Spence, Hugh Casson and a mysterious figure called Colonel Post, who although not a civil servant had an office in Sandys' ministry and seemed to know all his plans. The Duke of Edinburgh once asked me whether I knew Duncan Sandys' familiar. I did, for we had gone to the same school, which may have been the reason for my being invited in due course to be one of the three-minute speakers at the formal inauguration of the Civic Trust at Lambeth Palace; there were so many people invited to speak on that occasion that we had to keep it short. I remember making only one point, namely that for any scheme over a certain size only an architect under a certain age should be commissioned, which got me into hot water with the then President of the RIBA, Howard Robertson, who was sitting in the front row. He asked me what I had against him.

When Michael Middleton became Director of the Civic Trust things really began to move, with annual awards and great schemes in Norwich, Windsor, Burslem and elsewhere, so that we decided to invite him to stage an exhibition in The Design Centre, which Duncan Sandys opened. I kept in touch with Middleton and met him often as a member of the British Rail Environmental Panel. He was kind enough to suggest me to Sandys as a speaker at the Civic Trust's Silver Jubilee Conference in July 1982. I had very nice letters afterwards from both Michael and Duncan, but that was almost my last public appearance, for shortly afterwards I had my first stroke, but happily not such a bad one as that which was to overtake Duncan Sandys.

In 1966 I was invited to join the Design Panel of the British Railways Board under the chairmanship of David McKenna and the directorship of James Cousins. This appointment gave me a good understanding of the immense complexity of British Rail, but also of the great influence it could have on public taste. It also gave me the benefit of a free railway pass to any station in the United Kingdom. I was later invited to join

British Rail's environment panel under Simon Jenkins' chairmanship for a three year stint with Lord Esher, Sir Hugh Casson and Michael Middleton as the other outside members. The Design Panel thrived under Sir Peter Parker's chairmanship of British Rail for he really understood the importance of good design in a great industry and gave support to the idea. He once chaired a whole day's conference at which the Countess of Airlie, David Moroni and I were present as outside members. At this conference airing was given to the difference between marketing British Rail and running it, as the marketing fraternity had little feeling for British Rail's excellent corporate identity with its admirable alphabet, devised originally by Jock Kinneir and maintained over the years by the two directors of industrial design, George Williams and James Cousins, both former colleagues of mine at the COID. Design in British Rail was given a lift when by good fortune Jim O'Brien succeeded David McKenna as Chairman of the Design Panel, at the same time becoming a full member of the board. He set about re-establishing the standards originally set, paying as much attention to rolling stock as to corporate identity. One of his early activities was to commission David Carter to design a new locomotive for inter-city routes and another to commission Kenneth Grange to review the totality of British Rail design.

The International Council of Societies of Industrial Design (ICSID) was for me at least a marvellous excuse for foreign travel. Founded in London in 1957 it held its conferences and congresses every second year in a different city. The first conference was in Stockholm, and I gave one of the main papers, then came Venice, Paris, London, Barcelona and Ibiza and so on until the world had been covered. The London conference broke new ground because we decided to keep all meetings plenary and to invite distinguished people from disciplines other than design to talk on their own subjects, hoping thereby to educate the designers in the audience. We enrolled 900 members for the conference which was held in the Queen Elizabeth Hall on the South Bank. One of the highlights was a reception at Lancaster House, attended by Princess Margaret and Tony Snowdon and the then President of the Board of Trade, Anthony Crosland. I had personally raised a guarantee of £56,000 from British industrialists to enable us to compete with the excellent French conference of two years before. This we achieved, but the Spanish who had been elected the next organisers decided they had had enough high falutin' stuff and would revert to something much more simple—a sort of Club Mediterranée on the island of Ibiza; the congress preceding the conference had already taken place in Barcelona.

At the congress in Montreal I had been elected Hon. Treasurer of ICSID, having been a member of the board for a couple of years. I had resisted some fairly persistent efforts to draft me into the presidency, but at Montreal managed to get the rules changed, forbidding any non-designer from becoming president, an action which was to have rather painful after-effects in Dublin several years later, when Mme Josine des Cressonnières, the very efficient secretary-general in Brussels, decided to stand for the presidency. After much lobbying Yuri Soloviev, the Russian, was elected and Josine retired so hurt that she declared that she would never address another word to me, a threat she did not put permanently into practice. It was at the Dublin Congress that I was presented with the Colin King Grand Prix. I had persuaded Colin to attend the Kyoto conference, at which he was moved to make the generous gesture of endowing a grant to ICSID of £10,000 per annum. He died soon after and ICSID created the prize in his name. It took the form of a printed testament, designed in Ireland and signed by Kenji Ekuan, the President. It read: 'First awarded on the occasion of the 20th anniversary of ICSID at the Congress held in Dublin September 1977 to Sir Paul Reilly who, through his inspiration, example, enthusiasm and dedication, has made a unique and outstanding contribution to the understanding and appreciation of Industrial

Design throughout the world.' The presentation was made by Colin's brother Michael, with their father, Cecil King, sitting in the front row.

The Moscow conference in 1975 was, not unexpectedly, the largest ever. Yuri Soloviev had asked me to say some words of thanks 'from the West' at the end of the gathering, which I was glad to do. I still had to sum up the discussion of the group to which I had been attached, which was rather fun for I guessed that very few Russians spoke any English and I could therefore speak quite frankly as the simultaneous translations were totally inadequate. As soon as I sat down—to a good deal of applause from the Anglo-Saxons—I received a message from Yuri Soloviev cancelling my invitation to give the vote of thanks. I was not surprised, but later in the day I was indeed surprised to be asked by Soloviev to speak after all at the final session of the congress; apparently Gvishiani, the Chairman of the State Committee's conference organisers, had asked that I should. I kept it short but indicated that I had invented Soloviev in 1957. The final party was a very Russian affair with plenty of vodka, beer and wines from Georgia. At one end of the great room a long table, laden with special delicacies, kept the crowd of ordinary members of the conference away from the select band standing behind it; Annette and I were invited to go behind the top table to talk with Gvishiani and his attractive wife Ludmilla, the daughter of Kosygin, who both spoke good English. The next day we set off, together with some thirty or forty European conference members, for an Intourist tour of Central Asia—Samarkand, Bukhara, Tashkent and Alma Ata. The most memorable things about the tour were the constant laughter caused by the jokes of Eddie Pond, a one time President of the Society of Industrial Artists and Designers; the ugliness of the new buildings; the dirtyness of the hotels and aeroplanes; the poverty of the people; and the presence towards the end of a couple of KGB shadows—two men in mackintoshes and felt hats who followed us everywhere, even at the very end keeping our plane to Moscow waiting until they felt like embarking. From a height above Alma Ata we were able to look distantly into China, so although I have never set foot in that country I have observed it from both sides, for there was a similar vantage point in Hong Kong from which we got a closer view (Towards the end of my time at the Design Council I was invited to take an exhibition to the Chinese mainland, but, alas, this came too late for me.) We shared our British aeroplane back from Moscow with a party of rugby players and fans from Glasgow who on hearing the captain saying, 'we are now leaving the Soviet Union,' broke into happy cheering in which we joined.

12

New Interests in Retirement

Although I took no part in interviewing Keith Grant, my engaging successor as Director of the Design Council, there was inevitably a lot of discussion about the qualifications required for the job both among the staff and among the members of the Council. The contribution I liked best came from Lord Seebohm who had recently dined with us. He said the man chosen should have a wife who is a good cook. That made me think back through all the dinner parties that Annette and I had given over the years, each of which she had cooked, often without our guests being aware of it, and each of which had been a cordon bleu achievement; but then she had been well trained by her father, himself no mean cook, having served an apprenticeship, before pursuing his distinguished military career, in the kitchens of the Café Lucas in Paris. In due course Annette began writing about cookery, eventually becoming cookery correspondent for *The Times*, though unfortunately that was in the days before by-lines. An early dinner party set a pattern for many of our later gatherings for we had people from widely different walks of life—politics, art, music, the music being provided by a teenaged Julian Bream, the art by our dear old friend Barnett Freedman, the politics by Norman and Helen Bentwich with whom we spent many happy weekends at their cottage in Sandwich, and various industrial designers and their wives, about twenty people in all. Julian Bream, who played to us later in the evening, needed a foot stool, which we concocted out of four telephone books.

Later Barnett presented us with a print of a naked girl which we hung in our bathroom where it attracted some sixteen other nudes, all by friends of ours. His was the first Jewish funeral we attended, with an excellent address by Nicholas Bentley, while his obituary in *The Times* was followed up day after day by friends writing their memories of an unforgettable man. I think it was at Barnett's funeral that I first realised how many of our friends were Jewish, how many of them had come to this country as refugees and how many of them had made good. Arthur Koestler, whom I had first got to know before the war when we both worked on the *News Chronicle*, was perhaps the first, though we met again when he was married to Cynthia and enjoyed weekends with them at Denston in Suffolk; Annette was already a friend of his from her earlier marriage to Peter Lambda, the talented Hungarian Jewish sculptor. It was perhaps inevitable that, working for the Council of Industrial Design from the Festival of Britain onwards, I should meet a lot of refugees, for in those days the creative force in Britain was largely Jewish, a bias which became reflected in the membership of the Design Council, much to that organisation's advantage. I suppose if I was to choose one name out of the hundreds eligible it would be that of Sir Misha Black. I had known him, too, since before the war when he was living in Hampstead and we used to meet for drinks in the Isobar, the heart of Jack Pritchard's Lawn Road Flats. Misha, though not a first-class designer, was without doubt the most influential thinker on design of his day, an excellent lecturer and a marvellous chairman of any discussion. I was very proud to be asked by his widow to speak about him at his memorial service, held, perhaps surprisingly for a non-believer and a Jew, at St James's, Piccadilly.

Another thing that made me proud was my daughter Victoria getting herself into Fleet Street as a feature writer on the *Sunday Telegraph* where she did so well with her column on design that her editor suggested that she should go to Czechoslovakia to write about their glass and jewellery. It happened that my wife and I had been there for the Prague

35. Receiving an Honorary Doctorate of Science from the Lord Pilkington, Chancellor of Loughborough University, December 1977

36. Her Majesty The Queen and Lord Snowdon in The Design Centre

37. Her Majesty The Queen in The Design Centre, February 1968

38. Myself in The Design Centre

39. With Sir Terence Conran and John Stephenson at home on the day I joined them

spring and a week or so later for the Russian ultimatum to Dubçek and the arrival of the Soviet tanks. We had made several friends in Czechoslovakia while on duty there, so we were able to give Victoria some introductions, through one of which she met a young freelance architect and married him, thus ending her career as a journalist but starting a new one as a mother. We have never revisited Czechoslovakia and would not do so unless sent on a job, for we so much disapprove of their system that we would not spend our free Western money in their Eastern slave society.

I was, of course, quite pleased that Victoria should have married an architect, my sister, father and grandfather having all been architects and even I having been given honorary status as one. I still list my recreation in *Who's Who* as looking at buildings and was at one time a keen member of the Architecture Club and even a member of its committee. I joined when Lionel Esher's father was chairman and retired three or four chairmen later, but I never dared to speak in any of the club's admirable debates, though Annette did.

On the same day in June 1977 on which I retired from the Design Council, I joined Terence Conran and John Stephenson as a non-executive director of Conran Associates. The great office party they threw to welcome me helped me get over the pain of parting from my old colleagues and in particular from my two secretaries, Pat Francis and Hazel Sibley, who had looked after me for many years intelligently and devotedly. I brought to Conran Associates a great number of introductions for I knew almost every chairman of every large company and most were happy to accept my invitation to lunch with John Stephenson at the famous Neal Street restaurant which was partly owned by Terence. As the years went by, however, my value to Conran Associates decreased, for I found my friends retiring like myself and I did not know the new generation of chairmen. But I made up for this to some extent by accepting the Chair of the Conran Foundation Boilerhouse Project at the Victoria and Albert Museum. I had introduced Terence to young Stephen Bayley whom Terence appointed director. I was always anxious lest the Boilerhouse should somehow compete with the Design Council, though Stephen avoided this by careful choice of themes for his exhibitions and by showing foreign designs as often as possible.

But I was very depressed when I took Annette to Cornwall for a month's break after my retirement—a break rendered even more depressing by an accident to our little dog, Minko; he jumped out of the back of our convertible car and out of his harness and we found him a mile back with cuts on his face and gravel in his eyes; the Falmouth vet thought at first that he had broken his pelvis, but after a week in hospital he recovered. I wondered what on earth I was going to do, for Conran Associates needed me only for one day a week. I was grateful for any activity that would contribute towards my rent or even for one that could not, like the chairmanship of the Francis Kyle Gallery or of the Building Conservation Trust, John and Helen Griffiths' venture, which finally settled in Hampton Court Palace only a few paces from John's home. I was happy to have been asked by Bryan Montgomery, of Andry Montgomery Ltd, before I retired whether I would like to join him as a non-executive director of his subsidiary The Building Trades Exhibition Ltd which stages every second year the great exhibition 'Interbuild', now at Birmingham but previously at Olympia. I have seldom met such a lively group of people as those running Andry Montgomery. When I joined them they organised only the one exhibition. Within the decade they were staging exhibitions in every continent and on all manner of industries. One of my co-directors, until he joined the Government, was Lord Elton, the conservative son of the first peer, a Socialist, who wrote a letter to *The Times* of support for Ramsay MacDonald—a letter that my father had been asked to write, in exchange for which he would have been offered a peerage. In those days all peerages were hereditary so we had a hilarious time choosing a title for my father. We were staying at my grandfather's house at Upminster, so 'Lord

Upminster' sounded all right, but it never arose for my father refused to desert the Labour Party.

Two more little jobs eventually came my way—the chairmanship of Race International Design and a consultancy with Courtaulds. Race, one of Britain's leading furniture firms, had been bought by Ian Finlator who then had the idea that together with Professor Robert Heritage he should set up a design research organisation with me in the chair. It lasted several years and produced several excellent seats designed by Heritage. The Courtaulds consultancy was strictly to advise the chairman, Sir Arthur Knight, but I managed to travel the country calling on Courtauld plants and meeting their executives, as one of my ambitions had been to build bridges between Courtaulds and the Royal College of Art. I must have introduced up to twenty Courtaulds executives to the Professors of Textiles and Fashion over lunch in the Senior Common Room but, alas, without much result. At the end of my stint I thought back to an early meeting I had had with David Eccles when he was a director of Courtaulds. He had said that Courtaulds was too large to listen to me; what was needed was a number of small firms, each able to invest in new designs, without expecting the sort of return that a giant conglomerate would require. He had even suggested that, if I could find the small producers, Courtaulds might finance them.

One morning, when I was at Kintbury with Terence Conran and John Stephenson and the other directors of Conran Associates, Annette telephoned me at breakfast to tell me that a letter had come from the Prime Minister offering me a Life Peerage and asking for a reply by return. I thought she was pulling my leg and made her read it again. When it at last sank in, I began to realise that I need never again feel bored or unwanted, that I could always go along to the Houses of Parliament to listen or even to join in. But first there was the problem of my introduction. I had to find two barons to introduce me, for much as I would have liked to be introduced by Lord Caldecote, the Chairman of the Design Council, that was not possible since he was a viscount and a new peer must be introduced by two of his own rank. I therefore asked two former chairmen of the Design Council's Finance Committee, Lord Hayter and Lord Seebohm, if they would do it and to my delight they agreed, though I was rather sorry that the Design Council's public relations people missed the opportunity of publicising the event.

The introduction was preceded by a lunch to which Annette and I invited about a dozen people including my two chairmen of the Design Council, Sir Duncan Oppenheim and Lord Caldecote, and our doctor, Lord Hunt of Fawley, who had often told me how much he enjoyed being a peer, until sadly he lost his sight and balance and found it impossible to walk. The next event in the House of Lords for me was my maiden speech, a terrifying ordeal, but one which passed off without too much pain. I spoke on a motion by the Viscount Rochdale calling attention to the need to attract young people into industry. It was the second of two short debates, so the House was fairly empty when I got up to speak. I was surprised to be congratulated by several peers who spoke after me, but I discovered afterwards that this is a normal courtesy of the House.

Within a few weeks I was asked to join the Works of Art sub-committee, whose chairman was the Viscount Hood. In due course I succeeded him, but had to retire following a second stroke. I had, though, had the opportunity, as Chairman of the Works of Art sub-committee, of commissioning a marble bust of the Lord Home of the Hirsel to stand at the top of the Norman stairs with other busts of peers who had been Prime Minister. The sculptor was Michael Black, who attended the champagne party in the Royal Gallery at which the bust was unveiled. Other things I had a hand in were the restoration of the Chamber, particularly its recarpeting in a Pugin design of blue and gold, and the redecorating of four committee rooms and of the peers' guest room. I was very sorry to give all this up, but happy to hand it over to Lord Gibson.

I started this book with a reference to the house in which I was born. I shall close it by describing the house in which, God willing, I shall die. They were built within a few years of each other, my present one being a modest four and a half storeyed terrace house in South Kensington, actually in London's first conservation area. Its architect was George Basevi, Benjamin Disraeli's first cousin and thus one of the first of a long line of distinguished Jewish members of his profession. The attractive feature of these eight—four a side—houses are their first floor bay windows set in stucco below Cottingham balconies. They have gardens behind as large as the houses. I bought my leasehold for just over £2,000 in 1943 and shudder to think how valuable it has become; when our landlord generously offered each leaseholder an extended lease I did not have the £13,000 that would have secured me another fifty years, though my old aunt offered, too late, to buy it for us. Over the years we have filled the house to capacity, not with anything valuable, but with things we have liked, so that now there is no space on the walls for another picture and because I can never part with a book no empty shelves. We have owed a lot to the architects—not decorators—who have helped us remodel various rooms: Jacques Groag, who did one half of our bedroom, fitting clothes cupboards and a wash basin along one wall and on the opposite one a piece of fitted drawer furniture cantilevered from the wall and above that a long shelf on which my wife keeps her collection of small glass objects, most of them Scandinavian; Neville and Mary Ward, who knew Jacques Groag very well and carried on his shelving in the part of the bedroom in which we sleep in an Ambrose Heal bed; they also did our dining room with fitted veneered cupboards deep enough for one glass down one side, while Mary did our kitchen through the hatch. Wherever we have a flat top we have pieces of studio pottery, having started our collection with Bernard Leach, Lucie Rie and Hans Coper when they were easy to come by. All in all it is an overcrowded establishment, which has filled up year by year and is not likely to undergo any more changes, which is more than can be said of our neighbourhood; when we arrived some forty years ago there were plenty of small shops selling food and useful services—now they seem all to have become estate agents or banks, all useful no doubt, but not to us. We are, though, very grateful for our neighbourhood square, one of London's largest, best planted and richest in forest trees. Most summers it seems, my wife organises a garden party in it for neighbour to meet neighbour and dog to meet dog and to raise money for further planting—a popular and profitable pursuit.

I suppose I should conclude this book with a sentence or two about design as I see it today. I used to say sometimes in my lectures that design was like the budding, blooming and fall in nature or like the three orders of classical architecture, the Doric, Ionic and Corinthian, with the first and last phase running the risk of exaggeration and only the middle phase keeping its balance. I used even to draw parallels with other arts, with music or literature or painting or architecture, though they were seldom in step with design, painting being the pacemaker, with architecture close behind. I always opted for the middle phase, for the Ionic, since that was the most reasonable. This is well seen in lettering whether on the big scale, like shop fascias or the small, like magazine pages. But the superiority of the middle phase applies equally in every field of design, whether in textiles or television sets, furniture or motorcars; at one end things are too plain, too square and bare, at the other they are too decorated. When I joined the COID the market was divided, though certainly not equally. The commercial end was overblown and over-decorated; furniture, for instance, was fat and flatulent, plastics were bedizened and crudely coloured, and cookers were cluttered with details and engineers' art. At the other end of the scale there was a small segment of the market following the principles of the Modern Movement in Architecture. This Doric taste was certainly a relief from the commercial Corinthian, but it became carried to extremes, reminding me of the coloured

New York woman standing next to me looking in a shop window at a fairly skeletal piece of furniture who said, 'It is all right, but there is no love in it.' I like to think that by the time I retired from the Design Council there was some love, though not too much, in all that we showed in the Design Centre, whether soft or hard, craft-based or engineering-based. But outside the Design Centre, in the average High Street, nothing much had changed—indeed things had gone backwards; the shop fascias are all too large and garish and, alas, many of them have been designed by designers or rather designers who claim also to be marketing men; while what can be seen inside the shops makes me wonder what on earth I can have been doing during my twenty odd years in Haymarket.

What has gone wrong? No country has tried harder than Britain to improve design, no country has earned more praise for its efforts, yet few are in more need of achievement. I wrote something like that in 1948 saying that never before had so much lip service been paid to industrial design as in those post-war years. I then referred to an exhibition that the Council of Industrial Design had staged in Amsterdam and said that the COID had been particularly encouraged when a leading Dutch weekly had commented:

'The English section rises head and shoulders above the others. It is a joy for the eye to stay here among the teapots, irons, cigarette cases, books; besides the good form and good quality, one notices, to one's astonishment, that they possess a certain style in common, which is undoubtedly English. These objects speak of a modern civilisation. If you happened to see them in an exhibition in Nijni Novgorod, you would still know that they were English. Explain us the riddle.'

The explanation was, of course, that the goods shown in that exhibition, as in every other one staged by the Design Council, had been selected on two counts: first for their contemporary common sense and second for their membership of the

English tradition in design, a tradition of elegance rather than exuberance, of good form rather than high fashion, a tradition which was perhaps well summed up, in another context, on an eighteenth-century gravestone in a Hampshire churchyard: 'She (the lady of the Manor) was religious without enthusiasm and charitable without ostentation.'

So we could do it in our exhibitions and publications and we were not alone. The Society of Industrial Artists and Designers was in step with us, as was the Royal Society of Arts and the British Council and indeed any other body intent on improvement. For instance between 1947 and 1971 the SIAD produced seven admirably-illustrated volumes entitled *Designers in Britain*, which maintained very decent standards, whether in graphics or industrial design, while shops like Heal's and Dunn's did the same. And yet, in spite of these promising signs, this evidence of competence, we remained among the most backward looking of countries. This was always puzzling to me for, from my days with Venesta and my meeting with people like Wells Coates, Maxwell Fry, Jack Pritchard and Walter Gropius, I was convinced that Britain's future lay with the Modern Movement: nor did my sight of the 'Britain Can Make It' exhibition in 1946 or of the Festival of Britain five years later do anything to dispel that illusion. We were all set for modernism and I had joined the Council of Industrial Design at the right time. This euphoria lasted all my years at the Council and even gathered pace when we threw the doors open to engineers, for it was good to be able to show examples of high technology in the Design Centre to our ever increasing public and it was very good to watch the avidity with which the exhibits were examined.

But for all this, exciting as it was, Britain remained a retrospective place, with her shops filled with reproductions and her speculative builders offering versions of Tudor or Georgian make believe, while her local authority and institutional architects disfigured her towns with great lumps of building that were quite out of scale with their environments.

The reason for this sad state of affairs is that at all levels of education too little attention has been paid to design. We are a visually uneducated people who desperately need the Design Council which, thank God, now receives infinitely more money than it did in my day.

Apart from that, there are two reasons for optimism, two indicators that are poles apart in terms of design but which nonetheless give me cause for a belief that we shall pull out of the wood in due course. The first is the startling success of the Design Council in its work with the engineering industries, an activity I was proud to initiate when I was director; I had had the wisdom to appoint Geoffrey Constable to lead the attack. The second is the renaissance of the crafts, which has stemmed from the setting up of the Crafts Advisory Committee in 1971, of which I was in charge for seven years and which now as the Crafts Council with a greatly enlarged budget, publishes the excellent magazine *Crafts*, stages first class exhibitions in its splendid West End gallery and, as the Design Council used to do, takes the show on the road both at home and abroad. And not unexpectedly the Duke of Edinburgh intervened to give craftsmen a leg-up. He asked me through his treasurer, Lord Rupert Nevill, to help him organise a private dinner in July 1980 at Buckingham Palace; my part was to suggest half a dozen craftsmen to be invited to meet an equal number of the Duke's friends. I chose Victor Margrie, the Director of the Crafts Council but also a fine studio potter with work in the V & A; John Makepeace, the admirable Director of Parnham House, Dorset, which Prince Philip had visited on my recommendation, and a furniture maker of great originality: Professor Gerald Benney of the Royal College of Art, the well-known goldsmith and silversmith; Ivan Smith, the excellent blacksmith; and Philip Smith, the very skilled bookbinder. The purpose of the dinner was to see to what extent craftsmen were being commissioned by the laymen present who included the Hon. Angus Ogilvy, Sebastion de Ferranti, Lord Brabourne, Lord Porchester, Lord Zuckerman,

Lord Buxton and Sir Geoffrey de Bellaigue, Surveyor of the Queen's Works of Art. It appeared that there was a long way to go before these craftsmen could look forward to much patronage from the assembled company, but Prince Philip was quite right to test the market.

A more direct approach was perhaps one that I brought about first by introducing Lucie Rie to Wedgwood and later by putting Glenys Barton into touch with Sir Arthur Bryan, the chairman of the same company. Lucie Rie did not take, for her sort of studio pottery had little relevance to Wedgwood's normal production or at least Wedgwood could not discover any, but Glenys Barton had shared an exhibition with Jacqueline Poncelet at which both craftsmen were working in bone china one of Wedgwood's standard bodies. Arthur Bryan eventually came to see it and, just ahead of the Swedish firm Gustavsberg, signed up Glenys to work at Barlaston for a year doing anything that came into her head. At the end of the year the Crafts Council showed the results and very imaginative they were. Thus the Crafts Council began introducing craftsmen to industry, thereby reinforcing the work of the Design Council and thereby confirming my optimism.

INDEX

INDEX